BABY FOOD COOKBOOK FOR FIRST-TIME PARENTS

BABY FOOD COOKBOOK for FIRST-TIME PARENTS

Everything You Need to Know to Create a Healthy Start

Alexandra Turnbull, RDN, LD

ROCKRIDGE
PRESS

INCLUDES
75
RECIPES

For general information on our other products and services or to obtain technical support, please contact our Customer Care Department within the United States at (866) 744-2665, or outside the United States at (510) 253-0500.

Rockridge Press publishes its books in a variety of electronic and print formats. Some content that appears in print may not be available in electronic books, and vice versa.

Interior and Cover Designer: Francesca Pacchini
Art Producer: Hannah Dickerson
Editor: Anne Lowrey
Production Editor: Rachel Taenzler
Production Manager: Riley Hoffman

Photography © 2021 Elysa Weitala, food styling by Victoria Woollard, cover; © Annie Martin, pp. II, 56; © Laura Flippen, pp. VI, 20, 120; © Nadine Greeff, pp. X, 38; © Tara Donne, p. 74; © Evi Abeler, p. 94. All illustrations and patterns used under license from Shutterstock.com. Author photo courtesy of Katie Klingelhutz.

ISBN: Print 978-1-64876-935-1
eBook 978-1-63807-305-5

R1

I dedicate this book to my two beautiful children,
Brexley and Hollis.
May you always do what brings you joy.

Cheesy Tomato Corn Muffins

Page 98

Contents

Introduction

Hello! My name is Alex Turnbull, and I am so excited that you're here with me to learn how to confidently introduce solids to your baby. I'm a registered dietitian and expert in nutrition, but most important, I'm a mother of two. I know exactly how you might be feeling at this milestone: overwhelmed, nervous, confused, maybe all of the above. I've been there, too.

When I was pregnant with my first child, I panicked when I realized I had no idea how I was going to feed my baby solids—and I was a dietitian. Should I make my own purees? That sounded like a lot of work. Should I give my baby the same foods I ate? That sounded far from safe. I took my questions and turned them into my passion: educating parents on how to feed their families with more confidence and less stress.

There's a lot of parenting information out there, not to mention pressure from family, friends, random strangers at the grocery store, or the good old Internet. It can be hard to know whose advice to take, but whether you're starting with purees, taking the baby-led weaning approach, or some combination of the two, feeding a baby is really quite simple. The thing to remember is that even though what babies eat is paramount, the best thing you can do is create a positive mealtime experience. The rest will fall into place.

I've been through this introduction phase twice with my own children and have helped thousands of other caregivers confidently feed their babies. I'm here to hold your hand as a first-time parent or caregiver and guide you every step of the way. You're going to do great!

As a dietitian who specializes in infant and toddler nutrition, I'll be providing you with the tools and knowledge you need to properly and confidently nourish your baby. Not only will I explain everything, I'll also provide you with options so that you can discover what works best for you and the baby you're responsible for.

Together, we'll walk through the simple process of introducing solids. We'll cover topics such as knowing when your baby is ready to start solids, foods to offer and avoid at the right stages, portion sizes, and even the tools and utensils you'll need in your kitchen. Then after that, you'll find 75 quick and easy recipes to get you and your baby started.

Ready? Let's go!

Quick-Start Guide

If you've just been given the green light to start introducing solids to your baby but you're not sure how to get going, use this basic checklist to begin with confidence.

- First, make sure they are developmentally ready to begin eating solids. Check out the Milestones and Meals info on page 7.
- Next, make sure to read the Choking and Other Concerns box on page 6. It's important to familiarize yourself with what to do when it matters most.
- Then, pick one recipe. You don't have to prepare a feast for their first meal. Keep it simple. Try Creamy Avocado Puree (page 23), Quick Black Bean Puree (page 33), or Nourishing Quinoa Cereal (page 27).
- Determine one mealtime where you can provide a calm and positive environment, preferably a meal with the rest of the family.
- Get started! Offer a teaspoon or so of solids, either spoon-fed by you or preloaded on an easy-to-grab utensil (see Resources on page 122 for recommendations) for them to practice self-feeding.
- Enjoy watching them explore new flavors and textures and all the fun that mealtime has to offer. Don't forget to snap a few pictures of these precious moments and the funny faces that come along with it. You'll want to remember this.
- From here, simply follow their lead. Offer more if they are game and end the meal when they seem to have had enough. We'll discuss more of what this looks like on page 5.

Chapter One

Feeding Baby 101

This chapter will give you the tools you need to make feeding your baby safe and fun and will equip you with all the information you need. Take a deep breath and relax; by the end of this book, you'll be fully prepared. Remember the bigger picture: creating a positive mealtime experience for you and the baby you're caring for. And don't forget, you're going to do great.

Starting Solids

It may seem like just yesterday that you brought home your bundle of joy and now, suddenly, your baby is joining you at the table, ready to dig in at mealtime. Where did the time go? Just when you thought you were getting the hang of breastfeeding or found the right nipple for your baby to finally take a bottle, it's time to introduce solids. Where do you begin? You've heard so many different perspectives, opinions, and recommendations, but which is the right way? Truth is, there is no one perfect way to feed your baby. The most important considerations are providing a variety of safely prepared foods and a positive environment for them to eat those foods.

Everything you're about to read in this book will help you confidently feed your baby in a way that works best for you. Regardless of the abundance of unsolicited advice you receive from your mother-in-law, passersby at the store, or that intense mommy board on the Internet, you can rest assured that the guidelines in these pages will help you easily navigate when to start, what to start with, and so much more. As you begin this next chapter of parenting, remember to focus more on the time spent at the table together and less on how much or what they eat.

AGES AND STAGES

Most babies start solids at around 6 months. This is because the milestones necessary for a baby to safely eat solid foods develop around this time. Every baby is different. Start solids based on developmental milestones, which we'll discuss next, rather than a specific date.

Keep in mind that your baby won't immediately start eating multiple meals per day. The transition from breast milk or formula to solid foods takes several months. Also know that they may not eat everything you offer. This is normal; at 6 months old, a baby's stomach is only the size of a large egg. Although the foods you introduce early are important, breast milk or formula will continue to be their main source of nutrition through the first year of life. There's no need for concern if they don't clean their plate. Let them choose how much they eat. This will help minimize picky eating in the future.

Deciding which foods to start with can be overwhelming, but don't worry, most babies can handle a variety of foods from the get-go. You can always adjust as you go. Just be sure to enjoy this age and stage of your baby's life.

SIGNS OF READINESS

Most caregivers think that once a baby hits 6 months they're automatically ready for solids. This isn't necessarily true. Although most babies are ready around 6 months of age, some are ready sooner and others later. Avoid comparing your baby to others. Every baby is different when it comes to hitting these developmental milestones. To ensure your baby is ready to safely begin eating solids, The American Academy of Pediatrics recommends looking for these signs:

- Good head control
- Sitting up with minimal assistance
- Picking up objects and bringing to mouth
- Showing an interest in food
- Around 6 months of age

Once you know that your baby has hit all these milestones, you have the green light to begin introducing solid foods. For more information on when your baby is ready, check out the Milestones and Meals section on page 7. As always, if you have more questions on your baby's growth and development, speak with your pediatrician.

KEEPING IT EASY

It's likely that you've done an Internet search for how and what to feed your baby. From my experience, this can be extremely overwhelming. As a full-time working parent, I needed one spot to go to for correct and realistic information and a few great recipes in my toolbox. That's exactly why I wrote this book. I wish I'd had this book three years ago when I was in your shoes.

You don't have to spend hours in the kitchen just to feed your baby, no matter what the Internet might try to tell you. All the recipes in this book are simple and quick and will provide you and your baby with a fun new activity. And you don't have to make every recipe right away. Instead, try implementing one recipe a week or whatever you feel comfortable with.

Introducing foods to your baby should be fun! There's no perfect way to do it, either. Developing a healthy relationship with food starts with enjoying it—the taste, of course, but also how fun it is for your baby to rub in their face or hair or throw it on the floor. Although the mess may feel frustrating at times, know that this exploration is an important part of the process. Instead of micromanaging your baby at mealtimes, try to find the fun in watching them discover something brand new, like figuring out how a spoon works. And remember: Trays, spoons, floors, and babies are washable.

Baby's First Foods

Many caregivers think they have to offer foods in a specific order, e.g., vegetables first, otherwise the baby will never learn to enjoy them. This isn't true. The order in which you offer certain foods—grains, fruit, vegetables, dairy, and meat—matters less than offering foods safely and attentively. There's also no need to wait before offering a new food, unless it's a common allergen (more on this in Introducing Allergens on page 6). Restricting foods and how often you offer them can limit your baby's exposure to a wide variety of foods.

FOODS TO AVOID

The good news is that there are far more foods your baby can eat than not. Here are the few hard and fast foods to avoid per The American Academy of Pediatrics and the latest research:

Honey should be avoided until age 1 to avoid infant botulism. Your baby's digestive system cannot handle the botulism spores that honey is more likely to produce.

Cow's milk should be avoided as a beverage until age 1 to avoid competing with breast milk or formula. Other dairy products, such as full-fat plain yogurt and cheese, are okay to introduce before 1 year.

Added sugar should be avoided until the age 2, per the new 2020 Dietary Guidelines for Americans. Many baby food products contain added sugar that is simply unnecessary.

PORTION SIZES

Now that you know the signs of readiness and what to avoid, let's discuss setup and portion size. Start by creating a calm environment, preferably a time when you're eating, too. Next, place your baby in a high chair, sitting straight up. Finally, offer only a teaspoon of food to begin. This is where you smile and enjoy the moment.

Many parents want to know exactly how much food they should offer their baby. There's no specific amount, but rather as much as your baby wants. They may take just a taste, whereas other times they may seem to eat more than you. Babies are really good self-regulators. Let them guide if and how much they eat at each meal. You provide, they decide.

"But what if they don't eat anything? Should I force them?" The answer is no. Forcing a baby to eat can create pressure and a lack of trust at mealtimes, which can lead to more challenges down the road (hello, picky eating). If they turn away, start to get frustrated, or throw food on the floor, it's likely they're done. Remember, breast milk or formula will still be their main source of nutrition through their first year.

5

Choking and Other Concerns

Often the biggest concern for caregivers is choking. This was a big concern for me also as a first-time parent, but I learned how to safely prepare foods, which foods to avoid, and most important, I took a CPR class. It's important to stay calm during mealtimes, as babies can easily pick up on any stress we're experiencing.

When preparing foods for your baby, make sure to avoid offering hard, sticky, or round foods that can easily get stuck in their throat. Instead, try cooking or steaming hard or raw produce until it is super soft. Slice round items into quarters to decrease the risk of choking.

Many people confuse choking and gagging. Choking is where an object blocks the windpipe, so the baby will likely be silent. Gagging is actually a good thing. It is the body's natural defense against choking and presents with coughing sounds. Gagging is a part of learning how to manage solids. If your baby does start to gag or choke, avoid sticking your finger in their mouth to remove food or patting their back. This can lodge the food farther down. Instead, stay calm and let the baby work through it; if necessary, initiate infant CPR or call 911 if choking occurs.

INTRODUCING ALLERGENS

The good news is that most babies experience only mild symptoms if an allergic reaction occurs, such as a rash, diarrhea, or congestion. If one of these occurs, stop offering that food and contact your pediatrician. If your baby presents with severe symptoms, such as hives, trouble breathing, or swelling, call 911. Most reactions will occur within 15 minutes to 2 hours, so make sure to offer common allergens at least 2 hours before bedtime.

Research now suggests that introducing common allergens early and often can decrease the likelihood of developing a food allergy later on. The most common food allergens are peanuts, tree nuts, milk, soy, wheat, eggs, fish, and shellfish—and, most recently added, sesame. Safe ways to introduce common allergens include nut butter mixed into puree, whole-milk yogurt, omelet or tofu strips, canned salmon, and finely chopped shrimp. After offering one of these foods, wait three days before introducing a different common allergen to help identify which is responsible if a reaction does occur.

Milestones and Meals

Are you wondering at what point your baby can manage different size foods, utensils, or cups? Let me simplify the expectations and recommendations for you. But remember, every baby will be different, so these rules aren't black and white. As the caregiver, you get to decide when your baby is ready for the next step.

4–6 months: Baby will start to show signs of readiness for solids, including sitting with minimal assistance, good head control, bringing objects to mouth, an interest in food, and diminishing tongue thrust. Infant utensils can be offered, with little expectation.

6–7 months: Baby may be able to pick up extra-soft, long pieces of food using the palm of their hand (palmar grasp). They can start to practice drinking small amounts of water, breast milk, or formula from a small open cup.

8–10 months: Baby will be able to pick up smaller, pea-size food with their pointer finger and thumb (pincer grasp). They will likely be able to spoon-feed themselves at this age (but nowhere near perfectly).

12+ months: They will transition from breast milk or formula to cow's milk and should be eating all table foods, preferably what the rest of the family is eating. Offer utensils at each meal for practice. Start to transition away from using a bottle and move toward only open and straw cups.

Purees and Baby-Led Feeding

Have you been told you need to feed your baby a certain way? I'm here to tell you that the choice is yours. Many new parents are worried about doing it the "right" way, when in fact, there is no such thing.

The traditional approach that many caregivers start with is purees. Both my children's first foods were purees because it was easy and convenient. It's the potentially less messy approach and can easily meet all their nutritional needs. You can also promote self-feeding by preloading a spoon for your baby to practice feeding themselves.

The baby-led feeding approach has many benefits as well. You can offer some of the same foods the rest of the family is eating and avoid preparing separate meals. Research suggests that this approach can lead to healthier habits in the future.

The most common approach taken is a combination of both. I chose a combination with my children because I could pick and choose based on where we were eating and what was available at the time. At the end of the day, choose the approach that provides the least amount of stress for both you and your baby.

PUREES

If you're feeling unsure about which approach to choose, start simple with purees. Offering purees is a safe and easy option for your baby to manage their first bites. You can always thin the puree with breast milk or formula to adjust to your baby's needs.

Making your own purees doesn't have to be hard. Try one of the single-ingredient recipes from chapter 2 and alternate with store-bought options for convenience. (Check out page 11 for more information on grocery shopping for your baby.)

Worried your baby won't get the benefits of self-feeding if you opt for purees? No need to worry! You can still promote self-feeding by offering a spoon preloaded with a puree, set in front of your baby at mealtime, and watch them practice exploring a utensil. (For recommendations on utensils, see Resources, page 122.)

BABY-LED FEEDING (OR WEANING)

Baby-led feeding, also known as baby-led weaning, has been a very popular approach for caregivers over the last 15 years. However, I understand many caregivers are concerned about choking and whether this approach is safe. I was also skeptical at first. As I started to dig into the research, however, I learned that when offered correctly, baby-led feeding does not increase the risk of choking.

The times I did choose the baby-led feeding approach, it was convenient because my baby was eating almost all the same foods that I was. This meant less work and fewer dishes for me because I wasn't preparing a separate meal. I'll take that any day. Baby-led feeding also helps promote independence and develop fine motor skills, and it can decrease picky eating in the future.

9

Try, Try Again

You might find yourself discouraged when your baby isn't into solids as much as you are. This is common. They may need to look at it 10 times before they touch it, touch it 10 times before they taste it, and taste it 10 times before they eat it. Don't take it personally when they don't enjoy your award-winning homemade recipes. Instead, continue to provide small amounts of new or disliked foods with no pressure or expectation.

CHOOSE YOUR OWN ADVENTURE

Most caregivers seem to land on a combination of both feeding approaches. If you're wondering what this looks like for you and your baby, the answer is: however you'd like it to look. Try not to compare your baby's progress to another's. My children started solids at completely different times: one at 4 months, the other at 6. Some babies are totally content with feeding themselves from the get-go, whereas yours might prefer to be spoon-fed and avoid self-feeding until 9 months. If you find that your baby is refusing solids, it's possible that they're not quite ready. Take a break and try again.

Solids and Digestion

Here we are, talking about poop. Just when you thought you were getting the hang of what to expect in your newborn's diapers, solids changed everything. You may start to notice an increase in gas and constipation, as well as changes in texture, color, and frequency of your baby's poop. Normal poop should be soft and consistent in texture. If hard clumps or pebbles start to show up, your baby may be constipated. To remedy this, try increasing fluids by offering small amounts of water at meals and offer more "P" fruits (prunes, pears, plums, and peaches). Foods rich in color, such as blueberries and beets, can drastically change the color and smell of poop, so don't be alarmed. Instead, think about what your baby recently ate and whether it correlates with the color of their poop. If you ever see black, white, or bloody poop, however, contact your pediatrician.

Grocery Shopping

Loading your cart with store-bought baby food can quickly rack up the grocery bill. Save a few dollars and keep it simple by starting with foods you already purchase. For instance, buy bananas one week and simply mash a little for your baby. Add breast milk or formula to thin as needed. I loved making roasted sweet potatoes for myself and saving some to mash for my baby. Think about what you're already eating as a family that can easily be mashed or offered as a table food. Any seasoning can be offered to your baby, except salt. For foods you'll be sharing, add salt to the individual portions on the plate, rather than the whole recipe. All of this will save time and money. Who doesn't like that?

WHAT TO LOOK FOR

Strolling the grocery store aisles when shopping for your baby can be quite overwhelming. If you focus on everything you should avoid, pretty soon you're left with few choices and a bunch of guilt for what you did or didn't buy. Grocery shopping for your baby doesn't have to be hard. Remember, it's all food, just prepared differently.

When looking for safe and healthy foods for your baby, ignore all the claims and marketing on the front of the package and turn the product over to check out the nutrition label. First, take a peek at the ingredient list. The fewer the ingredients, the better. There's no magic number that automatically makes it "good" for your baby, and not every ingredient that's difficult to pronounce is "bad." Compare a few brands to see which one may have fewer ingredients and more fiber, protein, and iron. You can't win in every category. Consider taste as well.

Next, look for brands with no added sugar and minimal sodium. Don't worry if you can't eliminate these completely; just decrease as much as possible. There's no need to limit fruit due to natural sugars unless your baby is experiencing diarrhea. The nutritional benefits from fruit—vitamins, minerals, and fiber—far outweigh any concerns over sugar.

Do you really have to choose foods that are organic, non-GMO, antibiotic free, yada yada? Only if you want to. I'd rather your baby be exposed to a variety of foods, no matter the labels, than be limited because you can't find an affordable option that meets those high standards. Remember, you get to choose the foods that are right for your baby. If you need a simple place to start, fruits and vegetables are always a great choice, with or without organic, non-GMO, or other labels.

FIRST FOODS

Here's a short shopping list to get you started with the first foods to introduce to your baby.

6 MONTHS

- 1 bag of fine-ground baby cereal (oat, barley, or quinoa—avoid rice when possible)
- 6 sweet potatoes (babies love sweet potatoes; see My Sweet Lil' Potato Puree on page 36)
- 2 or 3 cans of beans (look for no-salt-added varieties or rinse before preparing)
- 1 bunch of bananas (easy to quickly mash yourself)
- 2 cans of light canned tuna (lowest levels of mercury and safe for baby to eat)

7–8 MONTHS

- Spices, e.g., cinnamon and garlic powder (not garlic salt)
- A few boxes of whole-grain pasta (try penne or rotini for easy self-feeding), or better yet, a lentil- or chickpea-based pasta (for an extra boost of iron)
- 32 ounces of whole-milk plain yogurt (great for practicing self-feeding with a utensil)
- 1 dozen eggs (try an omelet strip for a safe way to offer a common allergen)

THE "CLEAN FIFTEEN"

Ever heard of the "Dirty Dozen" or the "Clean Fifteen"? These lists provide insight into which produce items contain the highest and lowest levels of pesticides, but they may actually be more harmful than helpful. Just because you can't find the "clean" version of one of the 15 doesn't mean you shouldn't buy the fruit or vegetable. The most important thing is for your baby to try a wide variety of foods. Avoid passing on introducing a specific fruit or vegetable just because you can't find an affordable organic option. If you're dead set on organic, opt for frozen. Frozen fruits and vegetables are nearly as healthy as fresh, plus they don't spoil as quickly and are typically more affordable. Watch out for sauces and syrups that may provide unnecessary added sugar and sodium.

Stock the Kitchen

Good news! It's more than likely that you already have most of what you'll need to get started with making your own baby food at home. You don't need to rush out and buy every single kitchen gadget recommended on the Internet either. However, here are a few pantry go-tos, refrigerator and freezer staples, and handy tools that will definitely make preparing your own baby food easier. Remember, you don't have to get or try them all the first week. Keep it simple and start small.

PANTRY GO-TOS

Applesauce can be canned or in a pouch. Although great for on-the-go, prioritize spoon-feeding from the pouch or squeezing into a bowl for self-feeding practice.

Canned beans are an affordable protein that are also a great source of iron. Look for no-salt-added varieties or simply rinse before using.

Canned pumpkin is a simple option that requires little preparation. Add cinnamon and you now have a delicious and safe meal.

Canned tuna is a shelf-stable animal protein option that's full of heart-healthy fats. Look for light canned tuna in water to avoid any worry about mercury levels.

Cinnamon is great to add to any fruit puree, plain yogurt, or oatmeal.

Curry powder is a unique spice that is great to expose your baby to. Add to potatoes, proteins, and other veggies.

Garlic powder is an easy option to add to veggies and proteins. Get the powder, not the salt, to minimize sodium.

Nut butters are a great way to introduce allergens early and often. Spread a thin layer on toast or mix into oatmeal or yogurt.

REFRIGERATOR AND FREEZER STAPLES

Citrus fruits, such as oranges and limes, are an excellent source of vitamin C. Offer pureed, as a soft table food, or squeeze fresh juice into recipes (e.g., Quick Black Bean Puree, page 33) to help your baby absorb iron better.

Eggs might just provide the most bang for your buck nutritionally. Fry them, scramble them, or use them in recipes like Egg-cellent Asparagus Frittatas (page 80) once your baby is ready for table foods.

Frozen fruit, including strawberries and kiwifruit, is a great alternative to fresh. Try the creamy Banana-Avocado Freezy Pops (page 76) for a safe way to offer fruit that doubles as a teether.

Frozen spinach is a nutrient-rich option that lasts much longer than the fresh variety. Have fresh spinach that's about to spoil? No problem: Toss it in the freezer to use later in recipes, such as Superfood Spinach Puree (page 26).

Frozen steamer veggies are just as good as fresh, last longer, and are more affordable. Try broccoli, cauliflower, carrots, and green beans.

Whole-milk plain yogurt is a great source of calcium, vitamin D, and protein. Aim for the full-fat variety to promote brain and eye development and avoid the flavored options that are loaded with sugar.

HANDY TOOLS

Bibs: Silicone bibs with a pocket to catch falling food work great and are easy to clean.

Cutting boards: There will be lots of chopping in your future.

Grater: Great for shredding fruits and veggies to mix into recipes.

Ice cube tray: These work great for freezing homemade baby food for later (use silicone for easy release).

Immersion blender/food processor/blender: Blend together a few simple ingredients and achieve your desired consistency.

Knives: You don't have to stick to regular knives. Try a crinkle cutter for an easier grip.

Muffin tin (mini or standard): Use muffin tins to freeze homemade baby food (silicone works best), make muffins for easy finger foods, or use as a plate to serve your toddler's meals in.

Reusable/refillable pouches: Store-bought pouches are convenient, but try reusable pouches for your toddler to help reduce plastic waste and save money.

15

Sheet pans for roasting: Roasted vegetables taste very different from steamed. Change up the cooking method to expose your baby to a variety of flavors.

Sippy/straw/open cups: Prioritize open and straw cups over sippy cups when possible.

Steamer basket: Steaming raw produce is a great way to offer foods safely, whether pureed or as a table food.

Suction bottom bowls: These work well to minimize bowl or plate throwing. Rotate a variety of plates: sectioned, suctioned, and regular so that your baby doesn't get used to just one type.

Utensils: When spoon-feeding, use a soft-tip spoon, offer easy-to-grab utensils for self-feeding, and transition to the toddler version that's more "adult-like" with wide handles.

Vegetable peelers: Get rid of any hard peels on raw produce that make food a choking hazard.

About the Recipes

This book is jam-packed with everything you need to know to safely introduce solids to your baby, plus 75 recipes that make it even easier. You can use the information in this book whether you choose traditional purees, baby-led feeding, or a combination of both. As you start to pick out a few recipes you'd like to try, remember that almost all of them are freezer friendly. Make a little extra to save time later. (Time! Something I took for granted prior to having kids.) You'll also notice that you may have to experiment to find the best consistency for your baby. Easily thin purees with water, breast milk, or formula or thicken with infant cereal if needed. Stage one purees (for roughly 6 months of age) should be a thin consistency with no lumps—think slightly thicker than formula or breast milk.

Stage two purees will be slightly thicker, still with little to no chunks—think yogurt. Stage three purees will be thicker, with chewable chunks or chopped up foods. Avoid thick and sticky purees, like nut butters by themselves, as this is a choking hazard.

Not sure which recipe to make first? I get it; there are so many great options. I recommend keeping it simple with Creamy Avocado Puree (page 23), Quick Black Bean Puree (page 33), or Nourishing Quinoa Cereal (page 27). Start from there and add one recipe a week, or more if you'd like.

Avoiding specific ingredients to accommodate allergies, intolerances, and even certain lifestyle choices can make finding quality recipes difficult. Don't worry; I've included several recipes that are either gluten-free, vegetarian, vegan, dairy-free, or nut-free. With each recipe, you'll notice at least one dietary label to help you easily navigate which recipes are safe for you and your baby. I also include tips to make these recipes more nutrient-dense, flavorful, or easier to prepare.

TIPS

Some recipes include a tip with some extra information about the recipe. Look for these throughout the book:

BLF (Baby-Led Feeding) Tip: suggestions on how to present foods so that your baby can start to self-feed

Good to Know: any information that's helpful to you as a new parent or caregiver

Ingredient Tip: suggestions for handling an ingredient or to add more nutritional value

Pairing Tip: suggestions for foods or other recipes to pair with a recipe

Preparation Tip: extra help for preparing the dish, with the intent of making the recipes easier and saving you time

Variation: suggestions for varying a recipe or substituting an ingredient for flavor or allergy reasons

FOOD SAFETY AND FREEZING REMINDERS

Because a baby's immune system is more susceptible to illness than an adult's, good food safety practices are key to keeping your baby safely nourished.

How to freeze: Most purees can be stored in an airtight container in the refrigerator for 3 days or in the freezer for up to 3 months. When freezing purees, use an individual 1- to 3-ounce container, ice cube tray, or silicone baby food tray. If you use an ice cube tray or silicone baby food tray, wait until the cubes are thoroughly frozen, then remove them and place the cubes in a freezer bag. Don't forget to label and date the bag. Bear in mind that the longer a food sits in the freezer, the more the quality is jeopardized, so try to store foods where you won't forget about them.

What not to freeze: Although most purees freeze well, some foods don't do so well, such as raw veggies with a high percentage of moisture, e.g., cucumbers, celery, zucchini; fully cooked rice and pasta (make sure to undercook if you are going to freeze); and cooked eggs.

How to thaw: Take a small amount out of the freezer bag and thaw in the refrigerator or microwave. You can always take out more and quickly microwave, if needed; less is more. If using the microwave, make sure to stir and let cool to avoid hot spots. Because room temperature is smack in the middle of the temperature danger zone (40°F to 140°F), you should never thaw foods on the countertop, as this is the perfect temperature for bacteria to grow and thrive.

Food safety: Make sure to always wash your hands prior to food preparation, use clean surfaces and utensils, and cook meats to their proper temperature (poultry: 165°F; fish: 145°F; and red meat and pork: 160°F). Always reheat frozen foods to 165°F for a minimum of 15 seconds and allow to cool to a safe eating temperature.

Handling leftovers: When you start to notice your baby turning their head, pushing the food or spoon away, closing their lips, throwing food, or getting upset, end the meal. Don't insist that they take another bite, even if there's only a little left. It's important to recognize when your baby is full. Toss the leftover puree rather than save it, due to potential contamination from bacteria inside your baby's mouth. Any leftovers that have not come in contact with your baby's mouth or spoon can be saved for up to 3 days in the refrigerator. This is why it's best to start with serving less and add food as needed.

My Sweet Lil' Potato Puree

Page 36

Chapter Two

First Purees
(6-8 Months)

AWESOME APPLESAUCE

Applesauce was one of my son's very first tastes of solid food. You might be worried that if you offer fruits first, it will spoil your baby's relationship with vegetables. This is simply not true, so offer this naturally sweet and delicious puree to your baby with confidence.

Makes 16 (1-ounce) freezer cubes | **Serving size:** 2 tablespoons (1 cube)
Prep time: 5 minutes | **Cook time:** 10 minutes

DAIRY-FREE, GLUTEN-FREE, NUT-FREE, VEGAN

4 medium apples, cored, peeled, and coarsely chopped (about 1½ pounds)

¼ teaspoon ground cinnamon (optional)

1. In a medium saucepan with a steamer basket or insert, bring about 1 inch of water to a simmer. Add the apples. Cover and simmer over low heat for 7 to 10 minutes, or until the apples are soft.

2. Remove from the heat and transfer the apples to a blender or food processor. Add the cinnamon (if using). Blend until smooth, adding a few tablespoons of water as needed to achieve your desired consistency.

3. Cool and serve, refrigerate in an airtight container for up to 3 days, or transfer to an ice cube tray and freeze for up to 3 months.

BLF Tip: Raw apples can be a choking hazard. Try steaming peeled, sliced apples and offer your baby an easy-to-hold wedge. You can even toss in cinnamon, too.
Variation: Play around with using different apples (Granny Smith, Honeycrisp, etc.) each time you make the recipe. Different apples provide different flavors for baby.

CREAMY AVOCADO PUREE

Did you know that avocados are actually a fruit? Crazy, right? What's not crazy is offering avocado as one of your baby's first foods. Avocados were one of my daughter's first foods and I felt great about it because avocado has a safe consistency, is easy to prepare, and is full of healthy fats that are amazing for brain development.

Makes 16 (1-ounce) freezer cubes | **Serving size:** 2 tablespoons (1 cube)
Prep time: 5 minutes

DAIRY-FREE, GLUTEN-FREE, NUT-FREE, VEGAN

3 ripe avocados, pitted (about 1 pound)

1. Scoop the avocado flesh into a medium bowl. Discard the skins. Use a fork or potato masher to mash the avocado until smooth.

2. Serve immediately, refrigerate in an airtight container for up to 3 days, or transfer to an ice cube tray and freeze for up to 3 months.

BLF Tip: Avocado is also a great option to start baby-led weaning. Take a slice of ripe avocado, roll it in ground oats or flaxseed for an easy grip, and let your baby practice self-feeding.

JUICY BLUEBERRY PUREE

Blueberries are jam-packed with antioxidants like vitamin C that help your baby better absorb vital nutrients such as iron and fiber. You can also use frozen blueberries for this recipe. Just look for varieties with no added sugar.

Makes 16 (1-ounce) freezer cubes | **Serving size:** 2 tablespoons (1 cube)
Prep time: 5 minutes | **Cook time:** 5 minutes

DAIRY-FREE, GLUTEN-FREE, NUT-FREE, VEGAN

4 cups fresh blueberries

1. In a medium saucepan with a steamer basket or insert, bring about 1 inch of water to a simmer. Add the blueberries. Cover and simmer over low heat for 3 to 5 minutes, or until the blueberries are soft.

2. Remove from the heat and transfer the blueberries to a blender or food processor. Blend until smooth, adding a few tablespoons of water as needed to achieve your desired consistency.

3. Cool and serve, refrigerate in an airtight container for up to 3 days, or transfer to an ice cube tray and freeze for up to 3 months.

BLF Tip: Once your baby has developed the pincer grasp at around 8 to 10 months, you can cut blueberries into halves or quarters and let your baby pick them up and feed themselves.

Good to Know: Don't be alarmed if you try this recipe and your baby's diaper is a bluish green. That's from the anthocyanin found in blueberries.

COOL CARROT PUREE

If there's one veggie that most children enjoy, it's carrots. Because babies are naturally drawn to sweeter flavors, carrots are likely a veggie they'll enjoy for years to come. Pureeing carrots after cooking them helps your baby better absorb the beta-carotene. Offer pureed carrots at this stage, but know that baby carrots are a common choking hazard and shouldn't be offered until your child is at least 4 years old.

Makes 16 (1-ounce) freezer cubes | **Serving size:** 2 tablespoons (1 cube)
Prep time: 5 minutes | **Cook time:** 15 minutes

DAIRY-FREE, GLUTEN-FREE, NUT-FREE, VEGAN

5 medium carrots, peeled and coarsely chopped (about 1 pound)

½ cup water

1. In a medium saucepan with a steamer basket or insert, bring about 1 inch of water to a simmer. Add the carrots. Cover and simmer over low heat for 10 to 15 minutes, or until the carrots are soft.

2. Remove from the heat and transfer the carrots to a blender or food processor. Blend until smooth, adding ½ cup water (plus more as needed) to achieve your desired consistency.

3. Cool and serve, refrigerate in an airtight container for up to 3 days, or transfer to an ice cube tray and freeze for up to 3 months.

BLF Tip: Cut a few carrots the width and length of an adult pinky finger, toss with oil and garlic powder, and roast until extra soft before feeding.

SUPERFOOD SPINACH PUREE

Spinach puree may not sound super tasty to you, but it's a super option for your baby. Pair it with naturally sweet fruits and veggies like the Juicy Blueberry Puree (page 24) or Berry Green Smoothie (page 49). Leafy greens in their whole form are a choking hazard during the first few years of life. Offer them pureed for a safe option so that your baby can still reap the benefits that leafy greens such as spinach have to offer.

Makes 16 (1-ounce) freezer cubes | **Serving size:** 2 tablespoons (1 cube)
Prep time: 5 minutes | **Cook time:** 5 minutes

DAIRY-FREE, GLUTEN-FREE, NUT-FREE, VEGAN

1 (16-ounce) bag fresh spinach leaves

1. In a medium saucepan with a steamer basket or insert, bring about 1 inch of water to a simmer. Add the spinach. Cover and simmer over low heat for 3 to 5 minutes, or until the spinach has wilted.

2. Remove from the heat and transfer the spinach to a blender or food processor. Blend until smooth, adding a few tablespoons of water as needed to achieve your desired consistency.

3. Cool and serve, refrigerate in an airtight container for up to 3 days, or transfer to an ice cube tray and freeze for up to 3 months.

Ingredient Tip: If you have fresh spinach that's about to spoil, simply stick it in the freezer and use it to make puree for your baby or add it to baked goods, such as Two-Ingredient Pancakes (page 90).

NOURISHING QUINOA CEREAL

My kids now eat quinoa regularly, whereas I had no clue what it was until I was in my late 20s. Quinoa is a nutritional powerhouse. It's one of the only plant-based complete protein sources and packs a great deal of heart-healthy fats that are essential for your baby's optimal brain development. Plus, it's fun to say: KEEN-wah!

Makes 16 (1-ounce) freezer cubes | **Serving size:** 2 tablespoons (1 cube)
Prep time: 5 minutes | **Cook time:** 20 minutes

DAIRY-FREE, GLUTEN-FREE, NUT-FREE, VEGAN

½ cup quinoa, rinsed

1½ cups water, divided

1. In a small saucepan, combine the quinoa and 1 cup water and bring to a boil over medium heat. Reduce the heat to low, cover, and cook for 10 to 15 minutes, or until all the water is absorbed. Turn off the heat and let sit, covered, for 5 additional minutes.

2. Transfer the quinoa to a blender or food processor. Blend until smooth, adding the remaining ½ cup water (plus more as needed) to achieve your desired consistency.

3. Cool and serve, refrigerate in an airtight container for up to 3 days, or transfer to an ice cube tray and freeze for up to 3 months.

Preparation Tip: Short on time? Substitute precooked quinoa found in the rice section instead of making it from scratch. Find a plain variety to avoid any extra sugar or sodium.

EASY CHICKEN PUREE

With iron being one of the most important nutrients to provide your baby during the introduction of solids, chicken is a great go-to, particularly the dark meat. Give this simple puree recipe a try with your baby, and as you feel comfortable, add more ingredients for a variety of flavors and textures (for example, Chicken and Carrot Puree, page 40).

Makes 16 (1-ounce) freezer cubes | **Serving size:** 2 tablespoons (1 cube)
Prep time: 5 minutes | **Cook time:** 10 minutes

DAIRY-FREE, GLUTEN-FREE, NUT-FREE

3 boneless, skinless chicken thighs, cut into 1-inch pieces (about ¾ pound)

½ cup water

1. In a medium saucepan with a steamer basket or insert, bring about 1 inch of water to a simmer. Add the chicken. Cover and simmer over low heat for 7 to 10 minutes, or until the chicken is cooked through and a thermometer registers 165°F.

2. Remove from the heat and transfer the chicken to a blender or food processor. Blend until smooth, adding ½ cup of water (plus more as needed) to achieve your desired consistency.

3. Cool and serve, refrigerate in an airtight container for up to 3 days, or transfer to an ice cube tray and freeze for up to 3 months.

BLF Tip: Try slow-cooking the chicken thighs, cutting the meat into a long, ½-inch piece (roughly the size of an adult pinky) and allowing your baby to pick it up, suck on the juices, and feed themselves. The key to safe meat is making sure it's extra moist.

Preparation Tip: Defrost frozen chicken puree in the refrigerator, in a cold-water bath, or in the microwave. Heat in the microwave in 30-second increments, until heated to 165°F. Allow to cool and stir before serving.

28

PEANUT BUTTERY PUREE

With emerging research recommending the introduction of common allergens, such as peanuts, early and often, this is a great recipe to offer. Don't panic! Take a deep breath and start small. Give your baby a small spoonful of this puree, wait 10 to 15 minutes, and continue if you don't see any reaction.

Makes 16 (1-ounce) freezer cubes | **Serving size:** 2 tablespoons (1 cube)
Prep time: 5 minutes

DAIRY-FREE, GLUTEN-FREE, VEGAN

⅔ cup creamy, unsalted natural peanut butter

1⅓ cups breast milk, formula, or water

1. In a small bowl, combine the peanut butter with the breast milk, formula, or water. Mix until well combined.

2. Serve immediately, refrigerate in an airtight container for up to 3 days, or transfer to an ice cube tray and freeze for up to 3 months.

Pairing Tip: You can combine this puree with recipes like Nutty Sweet Potato Puree (page 55) or Nourishing Quinoa Cereal (page 27) at around 6 to 8 months or when you feel your baby is ready to try a slightly thicker texture. Try whipping the peanut butter, or other nut butters, with any fruit or vegetable puree.

BERRY BLAST SMOOTHIE

When looking for something sweet, I like to turn to nature's candy: fruit. Your baby will be drawn to this concoction and they'll reap the nutritional benefits while enjoying something naturally sweet. You can use this recipe as a puree, in an open or straw cup for practice, or poured into a popsicle mold for a nutrient-dense teething aid.

Makes 32 (1-ounce) freezer cubes | **Serving size:** ¼ cup (2 cubes)
Prep time: 5 minutes

DAIRY-FREE, GLUTEN-FREE, NUT-FREE, VEGAN

6 cups fresh or frozen mixed berries (blueberries, raspberries, strawberries, blackberries)

1 cup water

1. Add the berries and water to a blender or food processor. Blend until mostly smooth, adding a few tablespoons of water as needed to achieve your desired consistency.

2. Serve immediately, refrigerate in an airtight container for up to 3 days, or transfer to an ice cube tray and freeze for up to 3 months.

Variation: Swap out the water for formula or breast milk for a familiar taste, and add Superfood Spinach Puree (page 26) for an extra boost of nutrition and a fun new color.

EAT YOUR BROCCOLI PUREE

Broccoli is probably my favorite vegetable, so when it came time to offer it to my daughter, I was excited. I hoped she would love it just as much as I did, because I knew how great it was for her. But don't take it personally if your baby doesn't enjoy a food you love or prepare. This process takes time and many, many exposures. Don't give up! To streamline the cooking process, try using frozen steamed broccoli. It's just as good as fresh.

Makes 12 (1-ounce) freezer cubes | **Serving size:** 2 to 4 tablespoons (1 or 2 cubes)
Prep time: 5 minutes | **Cook time:** 10 minutes

GLUTEN-FREE, NUT-FREE, VEGETARIAN

2 cups broccoli florets, roughly chopped (about 1 large head)

1 tablespoon unsalted butter or coconut oil

¼ to ½ cup water

1. Cover the bottom of a medium saucepan with 2 to 3 inches of water and bring it to a simmer over medium heat.

2. Put the broccoli into a steamer basket or stainless-steel colander and set it over the simmering water. Steam until bright and tender, 5 to 7 minutes. Keep a close eye on it so that it doesn't overcook (when it is overcooked, it will turn an olive-green color).

3. Put the broccoli into a blender along with the butter. Pour in ¼ cup water and blend, adding more water, 1 tablespoon at a time, as needed to reach your desired consistency.

4. Cool and serve, refrigerate in a sealed container for up to 3 days, or transfer to an ice cube tray and freeze for up to 3 months.

BLF Tip: Roast with oil or steam fresh broccoli and offer a floret with a long stem for your baby to pick up and munch on. Make sure the cooked broccoli is extra soft and easily mashed between your fingers so that your baby can manage without teeth.

SPICED PEAR PUREE

Try an extra spice or two to take things up a notch. By simply adding a spice such as cinnamon or cloves, you're expanding your baby's exposure, which is one of the most important things you can do when it comes to feeding your baby. And remember, every baby step counts as progress.

Makes 12 (1-ounce) freezer cubes | **Serving size:** 2 to 4 tablespoons (1 or 2 cubes)
Prep time: 5 minutes

DAIRY-FREE, GLUTEN-FREE, NUT-FREE, VEGAN

5 small ripe pears, peeled
Pinch ground cinnamon
Pinch ground cloves

1. Slice the pears into quarters, removing and discarding the seeds and cores.

2. Transfer the pears to a blender and add the cinnamon and cloves. Blend until smooth, adding a splash of water, if needed.

3. Serve immediately, refrigerate in a sealed container for up to 3 days, or transfer to an ice cube tray and freeze for up to 3 months.

Variation: Don't just stick to one variety of pear. Try a different one every time you come back to this recipe or offer a combo all at once. Offering different varieties of the same food makes for great exposure.

QUICK BLACK BEAN PUREE

Beans, beans, the magical fruit—wait! Beans aren't a fruit; they're a legume. Seriously though, beans are magical when it comes to their nutrient profile. They're loaded with iron, which is a super important nutrient for your baby, and they have tons of fiber to help with the constipation that comes along with introducing solids. Add a squeeze of lime juice for more vitamin C to help increase iron absorption.

Makes 12 (1-ounce) freezer cubes | **Serving size:** 2 to 4 tablespoons (1 or 2 cubes)
Prep time: 5 minutes

DAIRY-FREE, GLUTEN-FREE, NUT-FREE, VEGAN

1 (15-ounce) can
  low-sodium black beans,
  drained and rinsed

2 tablespoons olive oil

½ teaspoon ground cumin
  (optional)

Freshly ground black pepper

1. Combine the beans, olive oil, cumin (if using), and pepper in a blender and pulse a few times, until well combined but still chunky. Alternately, mash the mixture with a fork until combined but still chunky.

2. Serve immediately, refrigerate in a sealed container for up to 3 days, or transfer to an ice cube tray and freeze for up to 3 months.

BLF Tip: Spread a thin layer of Quick Black Bean Puree onto a ½-inch strip of toast. If your baby is not ready for soft table foods yet, that's okay. Instead, place a small amount on an easy-to-grab utensil and let your baby go ahead with target practice into their mouth (and hopefully not the floor).

Good to Know: Rinsing canned foods can decrease the sodium content by up to 40 percent. Look for no-salt-added or low-sodium varieties and rinse before using.

OAT-ALICIOUS CEREAL

Although rice cereal tends to be the first food for many babies, it doesn't have to be. Many parents are concerned about arsenic levels found in brown rice. To ease your mind, just go with oatmeal. As a whole-grain option, oatmeal also contains protein and is fortified with iron. This recipe combines oats with water, but you can also try using breast milk or formula.

Makes 16 (1-ounce) freezer cubes | **Serving size:** 2 tablespoons (1 cube)
Prep time: 5 minutes | **Cook time:** 5 minutes

DAIRY-FREE, GLUTEN-FREE, NUT-FREE, VEGAN

½ cup old-fashioned rolled oats

2 cups water

1. In a food processor or blender, pulse the oats until you have a fine powder/flour.

2. In a medium saucepan, combine the oat flour and water and bring to a boil over medium heat. Cook, stirring frequently, for 3 to 5 minutes, or until bubbly and thick. For a thinner consistency, add more water a few tablespoons at a time. For a thicker consistency, continue to cook, stirring frequently.

3. Cool and serve, refrigerate in a sealed container for up to 3 days, or transfer to an ice cube tray and freeze for up to 3 months.

BLF Tip: Put a small amount of oatmeal on an easy-to-hold utensil, place it in front of your baby, and watch them try to aim for their mouth. Don't be surprised if they miss and it ends up on the floor. Embrace the mess!

Good to Know: Oats are naturally gluten-free, but they are often contaminated with gluten during processing. Look for oats labeled "Gluten-Free." Most babies do not have to avoid gluten, but family members may need to if they have an intolerance or celiac disease.

EASY PEASY PUREE

This might be news to you, but peas are not actually a vegetable; they're a legume, a legume that's loaded with iron, protein, and other great vitamins and minerals. They're a classic food to start off with for good reason. Instead of using canned green peas, opt for the frozen variety. This will ensure that you don't add any extra sodium to your baby's diet.

Makes 16 (1-ounce) freezer cubes | **Serving size:** 2 tablespoons (1 cube)
Prep time: 5 minutes | **Cook time:** 10 minutes

DAIRY-FREE, GLUTEN-FREE, NUT-FREE, VEGAN

1 (13-ounce) package frozen green peas

½ cup water

1. In a medium saucepan with a steamer basket or insert, bring about 1 inch of water to a simmer. Add the peas. Cover and simmer over low heat for 7 to 10 minutes, or until the peas are heated through.

2. Remove from the heat and transfer the peas to a blender or food processor. Blend until smooth, adding ½ cup of water (plus more as needed) to achieve your desired consistency.

3. Cool and serve, refrigerate in a sealed container for up to 3 days, or transfer to an ice cube tray and freeze for up to 3 months.

Pairing Tip: Although green peas have iron, it's not the most absorbable form. Try pairing with vitamin C–rich food such as citrus fruits, berries, sweet potatoes, or kiwifruit for better absorption.

MY SWEET LIL' POTATO PUREE

Sweet potatoes are one of my favorite foods to recommend caregivers start with. Their delicious flavor paired with great nutritional benefits are hard to pass up. If you don't have time to wait for the potatoes to roast, give them a few pokes with a fork and throw them in the microwave for 5 to 10 minutes, or until they're soft.

Makes 16 (1-ounce) freezer cubes | **Serving size:** 2 tablespoons (1 cube)
Prep time: 5 minutes | **Cook time:** 45 minutes

DAIRY-FREE, GLUTEN-FREE, NUT-FREE, VEGAN

2 medium sweet potatoes (about 1 pound)

½ cup water

1. Preheat the oven to 425°F. Line a rimmed baking sheet with aluminum foil or parchment paper.

2. Prick the sweet potatoes all over with a fork. Place the sweet potatoes on the prepared baking sheet and bake for about 45 minutes, or until soft.

3. Remove from the oven and let cool slightly. Use a spoon to scoop the cooked sweet potato flesh into a medium bowl. Use a fork or potato masher to mash the sweet potato until smooth, adding ½ cup of water (plus more as needed) to achieve your desired consistency.

4. Cool and serve, refrigerate in a sealed container for up to 3 days, or transfer to an ice cube tray and freeze for up to 3 months.

BLF Tip: Sweet potatoes are a great option if you're choosing the baby-led feeding approach. Simply peel the potatoes, cut into ½-inch sticks, toss in oil (plant-based oils, such as olive or avocado, work great), and roast until extra soft. Check out the Baked Sweet Potato Fries recipe (page 86).

**Lemony
Green Beans Puree**

Page 54

Chapter Three

Combination Purees
(6–12 | 9–12 Months)

CHICKEN AND CARROT PUREE

This classic combination is great for your baby, and you've likely already offered chicken and carrots separately. Give them a whirl together and don't forget to add some flavor with either the suggested garlic or whichever powdered herb you prefer. It's best to use chicken thighs as they are juicier and higher in iron. For a super juicy result, try slow-cooking the chicken.

Makes 10 to 12 servings | **Serving size:** ¼ cup
Prep time: 15 minutes | **Cook time:** 10 minutes

DAIRY-FREE, GLUTEN-FREE, NUT-FREE

2 boneless, skinless chicken thighs, cubed

3 carrots, peeled and sliced

½ to ¾ cup low-sodium chicken or vegetable broth or water

½ teaspoon garlic powder

Pinch ground ginger

1. Put the chicken and carrots in a steamer insert in a stockpot. Pour the broth into the pot, cover, and steam for 10 minutes.

2. Add the chicken and carrots to the broth along with the garlic and ginger, then puree by using a blender, a food processor, or an immersion blender with a tall cylindrical container.

3. Cool and serve, refrigerate in a sealed container for up to 3 days, or transfer to an ice cube tray and freeze for up to 3 months.

BLF Tip: Instead of offering cubes of chicken, which can be a choking hazard, throw the chicken thighs into a slow cooker with enough water to cover the bottom and cook until they reach an internal temperature of 165°F. Shred the chicken and give your baby a ½-inch strip of shredded chicken. It may seem counterintuitive, but larger pieces of soft food are easier for your baby to grab and feed themselves with—great practice for them and less work for you.
Pairing Tip: Pair with steamed carrots cut into ½-inch strips, and make sure the carrots can be easily mashed before serving.

CINNAMON APPLES AND PUMPKIN PUREE

Cinnamon, apples, and pumpkin, oh my! What a great combination that anyone would enjoy, especially in the fall. This recipe is delicious any time of year and is the perfect combination of flavor and nutrients to introduce your baby to a wider variety of flavors. Pumpkin is loaded with beneficial nutrients like vitamin A, lutein, and zeaxanthin to help protect your baby's eyes.

Makes 10 to 12 servings | **Serving size:** ¼ cup
Prep time: 5 minutes

DAIRY-FREE, GLUTEN-FREE, NUT-FREE, VEGAN

1 tablespoon lemon juice

12 ounces apples, peeled and cored

10 ounces canned pumpkin

1 teaspoon cinnamon

½ teaspoon nutmeg

1. Put the lemon juice and apples in a blender. Blend until smooth.
2. Add the pumpkin and pulse to mix.
3. Add the cinnamon and nutmeg and stir to fully incorporate.
4. Strain, if desired, for a smoother mixture.
5. Serve immediately, refrigerate in a sealed container for up to 3 days, or transfer to an ice cube tray and freeze for up to 3 months.

BLF Tip: Toast a slice of whole-wheat bread, cut into ½-inch strips, and spread with a thin layer of the puree. Untoasted bread can easily "gum" up in your baby's mouth and increase the risk of choking.
Preparation Tip: If you ever need to thin out a puree for your baby, try adding breast milk or formula. Make sure not to refreeze any breast milk that's already been frozen.

CHIA-MAZING PUREE WITH MANGO, PEAR, AND KALE

If there's one ingredient you can add to your baby's food that will instantly increase the nutritional value of whatever you're serving, it's chia seeds. This tiny seed can be sprinkled into nearly any food, especially yogurt, oatmeal, smoothies, and this puree. It's a great way to add a little extra without sacrificing flavor. I love watching how proud my two toddlers are when they get to sprinkle chia seeds into their yogurt.

Makes 10 to 12 servings | **Serving size:** ¼ cup
Prep time: 15 minutes + 20 minutes to sit

DAIRY-FREE, GLUTEN-FREE, NUT-FREE, VEGAN

1 mango, peeled, pitted, and cubed

1 pear, peeled, cored, and cut into chunks

1 cup kale, stems removed

1 tablespoon chia seeds

1. Put the mango, pear, and kale in a blender.

2. Puree until smooth.

3. Strain the mixture through a fine-mesh sieve, discarding any thick solids.

4. Add the chia seeds and stir to mix.

5. Cover the puree and let it sit for 20 minutes at room temperature before eating.

6. Serve immediately, refrigerate in a sealed container for up to 3 days, or transfer to an ice cube tray and freeze for up to 3 months.

Preparation Tip: Save time by purchasing full-leaf kale and removing the whole stem before chopping, rather than buying the leaves pre-chopped and having to remove the bit of stem from each piece.

CREAMY PRUNE WHIP

Once you introduce solids, you'll start to notice a change in your baby's poop, most likely fewer and more solid. This is very common, but still, many parents get concerned when the number of dirty diapers decreases. Although every baby's dirty diapers will be different, make sure to incorporate fiber-rich foods, like this Creamy Prune Whip, to keep your baby regular.

Makes 4 to 6 servings | **Serving size:** ¼ cup
Prep time: 15 minutes

GLUTEN-FREE, NUT-FREE, VEGETARIAN

6 prunes, soaked in warm water for 10 to 15 minutes

1 cup plain whole-milk yogurt (regular or Greek-style)

1 to 2 teaspoons ground flaxseed (optional)

1. Drain the prunes, reserving some of the soaking water. In a blender, combine the yogurt, prunes, and flaxseed (if using). If necessary, add a bit of water from soaking the prunes to get a smooth texture.

2. Blend until smooth.

3. Serve immediately, refrigerate in a sealed container for up to 3 days, or transfer to an ice cube tray and freeze for up to 3 months.

Pairing Tip: Mix this puree into oatmeal and yogurt for extra fiber and sweetness without added sugar.

Variation: Try freezing this mixture in an ice-pop mold for a sweet, soothing treat for a teething baby.

GINGER-IFIC LENTIL PUREE

If you haven't noticed yet, I love suggesting legumes as a first food option. Lentils will give your baby a great start with getting what they need to thrive, providing heart-healthy fats, fiber, and, most important, iron. To help better absorb the iron found in lentils, pair it with a vitamin C-rich food, such as the delicious My Sweet Lil' Potato Puree on page 36.

Makes 5 servings | **Serving size:** ¼ cup
Prep time: 5 minutes | **Cook time:** 30 minutes

DAIRY-FREE, GLUTEN-FREE, NUT-FREE, VEGAN

½ cup lentils, rinsed

1 cup water

¼ teaspoon ground turmeric

¼ teaspoon ground ginger, or 1 tablespoon grated fresh ginger

1 tablespoon coconut oil

1. In a medium saucepan, combine the lentils and water and bring to a boil over medium heat.

2. Cover and reduce the heat to medium-low, add the turmeric and ginger, then simmer for 30 minutes, or until the lentils are tender.

3. Remove from the heat and stir in the coconut oil until melted. Put the lentil mixture into a blender and puree until your desired consistency is reached.

4. Cool and serve, refrigerate in a sealed container for up to 3 days, or transfer to an ice cube tray and freeze for up to 3 months.

Preparation Tip: Cooked lentils are very tender, so pureeing this recipe is optional. If you prefer to soak the lentils before cooking (which makes them easier to digest and cuts the cooking time in half) cover 1 cup of lentils with about 2 cups of water and soak for 2 to 3 hours, then drain, rinse, and begin at step 1.

SAVORY BEEF AND SWEET POTATO PUREE

Here I am, talking about iron again. Beef just happens to be one of the best, most absorbable forms of iron available to your baby. This recipe is a home run with the addition of sweet potato for a vitamin C–rich food to help increase the absorption of the iron found in beef.

Makes 8 servings | **Serving size:** ¼ cup
Prep time: 5 minutes | **Cook time:** 30 minutes

DAIRY-FREE, GLUTEN-FREE, NUT-FREE

1 (8-ounce) beef sirloin, roughly cut into cubes

2 cups water

1 medium sweet potato, peeled and roughly chopped

2 thyme sprigs, or 1 teaspoon dried thyme

1. In a medium saucepan over medium heat, combine the beef, water, sweet potato, and thyme and bring to a simmer. Reduce the heat to medium-low and continue to simmer, covered, for 20 to 30 minutes, or until fork-tender.

2. Discard the thyme sprigs and allow the ingredients to cool slightly. Remove any extra fat, cartilage, or bones from the beef. With a slotted spoon, transfer the beef and sweet potato to a blender with about ½ cup of the cooking water. Blend until smooth, adding more cooking water as needed.

3. Cool and serve, refrigerate in a sealed container for up to 3 days, or transfer to an ice cube tray and freeze for up to 3 months.

BLF Tip: Try cutting the beef into strips and offer them to your baby to munch on and suck the juices from. This still provides them with some of the nutritional benefits. The sweet potatoes can be cut into wedges and roasted extra soft for easy self-feeding also.

CHEESY TOMATO AND CAULIFLOWER MASH

White vegetables tend to get a bad reputation, but let's set the record straight: Cauliflower is the best! Seriously, though, just because it isn't a bright color doesn't mean it doesn't deliver great nutrients. Cauliflower has a decent amount of choline, a nutrient that plays a large role in brain development and growing a healthy nervous system. Most people, including your baby, need more cauliflower in their lives.

Makes 4 to 6 servings | **Serving size:** ¼ cup
Prep time: 5 minutes | **Cook time:** 15 minutes

GLUTEN-FREE, NUT-FREE, VEGETARIAN

2 tablespoons unsalted butter

1 cup roughly chopped cauliflower

1 large tomato, roughly chopped

¼ cup shredded cheddar cheese

1. In a medium skillet, melt the butter over medium heat. Add the chopped cauliflower and sauté until tender, about 10 minutes.

2. Add the tomato and cook until soft, 2 to 3 minutes.

3. Remove from the heat and stir in the grated cheese until melted, then mash with a fork or puree in a blender.

4. Serve immediately, refrigerate in an airtight container for up to 3 days, or transfer to an ice cube tray and freeze for up to 3 months.

Preparation Tip: Just like broccoli, try roasting, sautéing, or steaming a long floret of cauliflower for an extra-soft table food for your baby to feed themselves, leaving you more time to feed yourself!
Variation: Other cruciferous vegetables, such as chopped broccoli or Brussels sprouts, are delicious in this recipe.

OAT-SOME PEANUT BUTTER CEREAL

Oats are a staple in our pantry, whether we use them in these creamy peanut oats, mix them into our favorite cookie recipe, or add them to homemade meatballs for healthy filler. This recipe doubles down on the nutritional benefits: iron-fortified grains and a safe introduction to peanuts. Plus, the banana will surely make this a favorite food with its natural sweetness.

Makes 4 to 8 servings | **Serving size:** ¼ cup
Prep time: 5 minutes | **Cook time:** 10 minutes

DAIRY-FREE, GLUTEN-FREE, VEGAN

1 cup water

½ cup old-fashioned oats

1 tablespoon creamy peanut butter

1 tablespoon coconut oil

½ teaspoon vanilla extract

1 very ripe banana, mashed (optional)

1. In a medium saucepan, bring the water to a boil. Add the oats and return to a boil, then reduce the heat to low and cover.

2. Cook until your desired texture is reached. Stir in the peanut butter, coconut oil, vanilla, and mashed banana (if using).

3. Cool and serve, or refrigerate in a sealed container for up to 3 days.

Good to Know: Peanut butter can often be a source of added sugars. Look for a variety without added sugar. If this isn't your preferred brand, purchase a separate one for your baby and give it a try every once in a while to help "train" your palate to a healthier option.

PEACHY KALE-TOFU PUREE

Tofu is a great option for introducing to baby as one of their first foods. It's a complete plant-based protein, contains iron and calcium, and is a safe way to introduce soy, a common allergen. If you're not used to preparing tofu, it can be intimidating. Incorporating tofu into your baby's diet is really quite easy and, when adding the right flavors, really yummy.

Makes 4 servings | **Serving size:** ¼ cup
Prep time: 5 minutes | **Cook time:** 5 minutes

DAIRY-FREE, NUT-FREE, VEGAN

2 cups torn fresh kale leaves

1 medium peach, pitted and peeled

¼ cup diced firm tofu

1. Fill a medium saucepan with about 1 inch of water and bring to a simmer. Place the kale in a steamer basket, set it over the simmering water, cover, and cook until tender, about 5 minutes. Allow to cool.

2. Slice the peach into 1-inch chunks.

3. In a blender or food processor, puree the cooled kale, peach, and tofu until the mixture reaches your desired consistency. Add water, if necessary.

4. Serve immediately, refrigerate in a sealed container for up to 3 days, or transfer to an ice cube tray and freeze for up to 3 months.

BLF Tip: Once you're ready to introduce tofu as a soft table food to your baby, try Baked Tofu with Sesame Dipping Sauce (page 89).

BERRY GREEN SMOOTHIE

One thing that makes me cringe is tossing spoiled food, including fresh produce and yogurt. Making smoothies is a great way to use up what you have, decrease food waste, and offer your baby a ton of nutrition all in one cup. Try purchasing frozen spinach and berries for a longer shelf life; they're also easier on your pocketbook and still contain all the benefits of fresh versions.

Makes 8 servings | **Serving size:** ¼ cup
Prep time: 10 minutes

GLUTEN-FREE, NUT-FREE, VEGETARIAN

½ cup baby spinach

½ cup fresh or frozen mixed berries

½ cup full-fat plain yogurt

1 cup whole milk (soy or almond milk can be substituted)

1. In a blender or food processor, combine the spinach, berries, yogurt, and milk and puree until smooth.

2. Serve immediately, refrigerate in a sealed container for up to 3 days, or transfer to an ice cube tray and freeze for up to 3 months.

Variation: Pour into popsicle molds and freeze until solid to make this smoothie a fun new option. Smoothie popsicles are a great choice when your baby is teething.

COMBINATION PUREES (6–12 | 9–12 MONTHS)

BEEFY ASPARAGUS-PEAR PUREE

This recipe is easy to make and hits nearly every important nutrient, specifically iron, without the confusion. Plus, this recipe gets you out of the rut of offering the traditional vegetables, such as peas, carrots, and potatoes. Exposure to a variety of foods is one of the key components of developing a healthy relationship with food.

Makes 4 servings | **Serving size:** ¼ cup
Prep time: 5 minutes | **Cook time:** 15 minutes

DAIRY-FREE, GLUTEN-FREE, NUT-FREE

1 large pear, peeled

1 cup trimmed asparagus spears

½ pound ground beef

1. Cut the pear into 1-inch chunks.

2. Fill a medium saucepan with about 1 inch of water and bring to a simmer. Place the pear and asparagus in a steamer basket, set it over the simmering water, cover, and cook until tender, about 8 minutes. Allow to cool.

3. While the asparagus and pears are steaming, in a medium sauté pan or skillet, cook the ground beef over medium-low heat, stirring frequently and breaking the beef into small pieces with a spoon as it browns, for about 15 minutes, until browned evenly and cooked through.

4. Drain the excess fat from the pan and allow the beef to cool.

5. In a blender or food processor, puree the cooled beef, pears, and asparagus until your desired consistency is reached. Add water, if necessary.

6. Serve immediately, refrigerate in a sealed container for up to 3 days, or transfer to an ice cube tray and freeze for up to 3 months.

BLF Tip: Asparagus is a great baby-led feeding option. Simply sauté, roast, or steam it until it is extra soft. The natural shape of an asparagus spear makes it easy for your baby to pick up and munch on.

CHUNKY CARROTS AND BROCCOLI WITH GINGER PUREE

Don't assume your baby won't like vegetables. This mindset can set you up for failure, and we don't want that. Be open-minded and give this delicious ginger-infused recipe a try. The combination of vitamins and minerals from broccoli and carrots, paired with the infection-fighting benefits of ginger, make it a no-brainer to serve this to your baby to protect their health.

Makes 32 (1-ounce) freezer cubes | **Serving size:** ¼ cup (2 cubes)
Prep time: 10 minutes | **Cook time:** 15 minutes

DAIRY-FREE, GLUTEN-FREE, NUT-FREE, VEGAN

5 medium carrots, peeled and coarsely chopped (about 1 pound)

1 medium head broccoli, coarsely chopped (about 1 pound)

1 tablespoon finely chopped ginger

1 cup water

1. In a medium saucepan with a steamer basket or insert, bring about 1 inch of water to a simmer. Add the carrots and broccoli. Cover and simmer over low heat for 10 to 15 minutes, or until the carrots and broccoli are soft.

2. Remove from the heat and transfer the carrots and broccoli to a blender or food processor. Add the ginger. Blend until mostly smooth, adding the water (plus more as needed) to achieve your desired consistency.

3. Cool and serve, refrigerate in a sealed container for up to 3 days, or transfer to an ice cube tray and freeze for up to 3 months.

BLF Tip: Broccoli and carrots were two of my favorite vegetables to offer as a soft table food to my children from the get-go. Roast, sauté, or steam a large, "stick-like" portion and add your favorite seasonings, such as ginger for an extra flavor boost.

MASHED KIWIFRUIT AND BANANA

Banana is a classic first food to offer to a baby, but kiwifruit is also wonderful. This recipe is a great example of combining a familiar food with a less commonly used option to provide variety. Kiwifruit offers up a powerful punch of vitamin C and fiber to benefit your baby.

Makes 32 (1-ounce) freezer cubes | **Serving size:** ¼ cup (2 cubes)
Prep time: 5 minutes

DAIRY-FREE, GLUTEN-FREE, NUT-FREE, VEGAN

6 kiwifruit, halved and flesh removed with a spoon

3 bananas

1. Combine the kiwifruit and bananas in a medium bowl. Mash with a fork until mostly smooth.

2. Serve immediately, refrigerate in a sealed container for up to 3 days, or transfer to an ice cube tray and freeze for up to 3 months.

BLF Tip: Both kiwifruit and banana can be offered with a portion of the peel left on for an easy pick up and grip. Without the bit of peel, they can be quite slippery and difficult for your baby to eat, let alone get a taste.

LEMONY GREEN BEANS PUREE

My daughter was never a fan of green beans until she turned 3. We introduced them from the beginning and never gave up. Over time, with many exposures, she grew to love them. Instead of offering green beans plain, without any flavor, add something simple, such as lemon juice, to make them more exciting. Adding a bit of extra flavor will be a key strategy to help your children enjoy a wide variety of foods.

Makes 32 (1-ounce) freezer cubes | **Serving size:** ¼ cup (2 cubes)
Prep time: 5 minutes | **Cook time:** 15 minutes

DAIRY-FREE, GLUTEN-FREE, NUT-FREE, VEGAN

2 pounds green beans, trimmed

Juice of ½ lemon (about 1 tablespoon)

Zest of ½ lemon (about 1 teaspoon)

½ cup water

1. In a medium saucepan with a steamer basket or insert, bring about 1 inch of water to a simmer. Add the green beans. Cover and simmer over low heat for 10 to 15 minutes, or until the green beans are soft.

2. Remove from the heat and transfer the green beans to a blender or food processor. Add the lemon juice and lemon zest. Blend until mostly smooth, adding the water (plus more as needed) to achieve your desired consistency.

3. Cool and serve, refrigerate in a sealed container for up to 3 days, or transfer to an ice cube tray and freeze for up to 3 months.

BLF Tip: If you find that your baby is having a hard time managing chunks of food, don't give up; this is a new texture for them. You can also provide soft table foods to see if this is their preferred texture. Sometimes the combination of chunks and puree can confuse them.
Variation: If you don't want to deal with trimming fresh green beans, use frozen green beans steamed in the microwave.

54

NUTTY SWEET POTATO PUREE

The latest research recommends offering common allergens, such as peanuts, early and often. Although peanuts in their whole form are a choking hazard, offering them as a nut butter pureed into a low-allergenic food like sweet potatoes is a delicious way to safely introduce them.

Makes 4 servings | **Serving size:** ¼ cup
Prep time: 5 minutes | **Cook time:** 20 minutes

DAIRY-FREE, GLUTEN-FREE, VEGAN

- **1 medium to large sweet potato (about 1 pound), peeled and diced into 1-inch chunks**
- **1 to 2 teaspoons creamy nut butter (peanut, almond, or cashew) or tahini**

1. Cover the bottom of a medium saucepan with 2 to 3 inches of water and bring it to a simmer over medium heat.

2. Put the sweet potato chunks into a steamer basket or stainless-steel colander and set it over the simmering water. Steam for 15 to 20 minutes, or until soft. Allow to cool slightly.

3. Combine the sweet potato and nut butter in a blender along with enough water to make a smooth mixture. Alternatively, mash the sweet potato and nut butter with a fork until combined.

4. Cool and serve, refrigerate in a sealed container for up to 3 days, or transfer to an ice cube tray and freeze for up to 3 months.

Preparation Tip: Sweet potatoes tend to puree into a thick texture. If you need something a bit thinner for your baby, try adding breast milk or formula to create the appropriate texture while adding a familiar boost of calories.
Variation: Try another nut butter, other than peanut, such as almond or cashew.

Baby Guacamole

Page 64

Chapter Four

Next-Level Purees
(6–12 | 9–12 Months)

CHERRY-LICIOUS PORK AND PEAR PUREE

When you think of baby food, cherries may not be the first ingredient that comes to mind. However, this recipe has the perfect flavor combination to train your baby to have a diverse palate. Your baby will love the taste and you'll feel great providing them with an essential group of nutrients, including protein, iron, antioxidants, and vitamin C.

Makes 5 servings | **Serving size:** ¼ cup
Prep time: 5 minutes | **Cook time:** 10 minutes

DAIRY-FREE, GLUTEN-FREE, NUT-FREE

1 medium pear, cored and peeled

½ cup cherries, pitted and halved

½ cup diced cooked pork loin

1. Cut the pear into ½-inch cubes.

2. Fill a medium saucepan with about 1 inch of water and bring to a simmer. Place the pear and cherries in a steamer basket and set it over the simmering water. Cover and cook until tender when pierced with a fork or knife, 8 to 10 minutes. Allow to cool.

3. In a blender or food processor, puree the cooled cherries and pear and the pork until your desired consistency is reached. Add water, if necessary.

4. Cool and serve, refrigerate in an airtight container for up to 3 days, or transfer to an ice cube tray and freeze for up to 3 months.

Ingredient Tip: Instead of waiting for your fresh pears to ripen, save time and opt for canned pears in water or 100-percent juice. Avoid the varieties packed in syrup, including the light varieties.

58

REFRESHING TURKEY, MANGO, AND CUCUMBER PUREE

This delightfully refreshing puree will give your baby a healthy dose of vitamin C. When introducing solids, vitamin C–rich foods play a vital role, specifically in iron absorption and immunity. Additionally, the olive oil in this recipe will help your baby better absorb vitamins A, D, E, and K. This recipe is all about optimizing your baby's absorption of nutrients.

Makes 4 servings | **Serving size:** ¼ cup
Prep time: 5 minutes | **Cook time:** 15 minutes

DAIRY-FREE, GLUTEN-FREE, NUT-FREE

1 teaspoon olive oil

½ pound ground turkey

½ cup cubed mango

½ cup cucumber, peeled and cubed

1. In a medium sauté pan or skillet, heat the olive oil over medium heat.

2. Add the ground turkey and reduce the heat to medium-low. Cook, stirring frequently and breaking up the turkey into small pieces with a spoon as it browns, for about 15 minutes, until browned evenly and cooked through.

3. Drain the excess fat from the pan and allow the turkey to cool.

4. In a blender or food processor, combine the cooled turkey, mango, and cucumber and puree until your desired consistency is reached. Add water, if necessary.

5. Cool and serve, refrigerate in an airtight container for up to 3 days, or transfer to an ice cube tray and freeze for up to 3 months.

CREAMY WHITE BEANS AND SPINACH PUREE

This creamy recipe has no dairy. Instead, the cooked and mashed beans help create a creamy consistency that, when paired with garlic and onion, is just wonderful. If you have fresh spinach you'd like to use up before it spoils or simply because that's what you prefer, go ahead and use that instead of the frozen. Just double the volume and finely chop for an equivalent result.

Makes 30 (1-ounce) freezer cubes | **Serving size:** ¼ cup (2 cubes)
Prep time: 5 minutes | **Cook time:** 10 minutes

DAIRY-FREE, GLUTEN-FREE, NUT-FREE, VEGAN

1 tablespoon olive oil

1 onion, finely chopped

1 (15-ounce can) low-sodium great northern or cannellini beans, drained and rinsed

½ cup water

½ teaspoon garlic powder

2 (10-ounce) packages frozen chopped spinach, defrosted and squeezed to remove excess water

1. In a medium skillet over medium-low heat, heat the olive oil. Add the onion and cook for 5 to 7 minutes, stirring frequently to prevent browning, until the onion has softened.

2. Add the beans, water, and garlic powder to the skillet. Mash and stir the beans until mostly smooth, adding a few additional tablespoons of water as needed to achieve your desired consistency.

3. Add the spinach to the bean mixture and stir to combine. Cook for 1 to 2 minutes, or until the spinach is heated through.

4. Cool and serve, refrigerate in an airtight container for up to 3 days, or transfer to an ice cube tray and freeze for up to 3 months.

Pairing Tip: This recipe goes great with Chicken and Carrot Puree (page 40).

BEEF AND ROOT VEGGIE PUREE

You can't go wrong with this classic dish on a cold winter day. I remember my mom making stew and the amazing aromas it spread throughout the house. Get this cooking in your kitchen and allow your baby to use all of their senses with this stew-inspired puree, starting with their nose.

Makes 32 (1-ounce) freezer cubes | **Serving size:** ¼ cup (2 cubes)
Prep time: 10 minutes | **Cook time:** 4 to 8 hours

DAIRY-FREE, GLUTEN-FREE, NUT-FREE

1½ pounds stew beef, cut into 1½-inch pieces

1 pound assorted root vegetables (carrots, parsnips, sweet potatoes, turnips, rutabaga), peeled and cut into 1-inch pieces

½ teaspoon dried thyme

½ teaspoon dried rosemary

In a slow cooker, place the beef, vegetables, thyme, and rosemary. Add enough water to halfway cover the vegetables and meat.

Cover and cook on high for 4 hours or low for 8 hours, until the meat is tender and shreds easily with a fork.

Transfer the meat to a bowl, leaving the vegetables and liquid in the slow cooker. Shred the beef into small pieces. Transfer the vegetables and ½ cup of the cooking liquid to the bowl with the meat. Use a fork or potato masher to mash and mix the vegetables with the beef until mostly smooth, adding a few additional tablespoons of cooking liquid as needed to achieve your desired consistency. Reserve the remaining cooking liquid for another use.

Cool and serve, refrigerate in an airtight container for up to 2 days, or transfer to an ice cube tray and freeze for up to 2 months.

BLF Tip: Cooking the beef in a slow cooker will produce the most tender meat, which is best when offering whole pieces for self-feeding. The goal is to make the meat as moist and soft as possible, to make it easier for baby to eat.

GO-GO GREEN FRUIT AND VEG PUREE

Sometimes straight-up spinach just won't do. In order to help balance out the mild flavor, pairing spinach with a few fruits is guaranteed to be a crowd-pleaser. The coconut water in this recipe helps provide an extra-hydrating boost, but make sure to avoid sweetened varieties.

Makes 32 (1-ounce) freezer cubes | **Serving size:** ¼ cup (2 cubes)
Prep time: 15 minutes

DAIRY-FREE, GLUTEN-FREE, VEGAN

1 Bartlett pear, peeled, cored, and quartered

1 cup steamed sweet peas

1 cup spinach, stems trimmed

2 kiwifruit, peeled, quartered, and white pith removed from center

4 ounces coconut water, plus more if desired

1. Place the pear, peas, spinach, and kiwifruit in a blender.

2. Blend and puree until smooth, adding a little coconut water at a time to achieve your desired consistency.

3. Strain, if desired, for a smoother texture.

4. Serve immediately, refrigerate in an airtight container for up to 3 days, or transfer to an ice cube tray and freeze for up to 3 months.

Good to Know: By now, you may be used to pulverizing the heck out of ingredients. At this point, it's likely okay to leave the puree a little chunkier or move on to soft table foods so that your baby can work on tolerating additional textures.

HEARTY CHICKEN AND VEGGIE STEW

This hearty chicken casserole is sure to be loved by the whole family. It's also easy enough to swap out the carrots, potatoes, and parsnips for whatever root vegetables you have on hand. The leeks are a great new addition for your baby, but if you don't have any, you can use chopped onions instead.

Makes 10 to 12 servings | **Serving size:** ¼ cup
Prep time: 10 minutes | **Cook time:** 25 minutes

DAIRY-FREE, GLUTEN-FREE, NUT-FREE

1 tablespoon olive oil

2 carrots, peeled and chopped

⅔ cup sliced leeks, white part only, washed

¼ pound boneless, skinless chicken breast, cut into 2-inch chunks

1 teaspoon chopped fresh herbs (such as rosemary, thyme, or parsley)

2 potatoes, peeled and chopped

1 parsnip, peeled and chopped

1. In a medium saucepan, heat the olive oil over medium heat. Add the carrots and leeks. Sauté until the vegetables have softened, about 5 minutes. Add the chicken and herbs to the pan, sautéing for 5 to 7 minutes, or until the chicken is lightly browned and the internal temperature reaches 165°F.

2. Add the potatoes, parsnip, and enough water to just cover the contents of the pan. Cover and simmer for about 15 minutes, or until everything is fork-tender. Transfer all the ingredients to a blender and puree until your desired consistency is reached, adding more water as necessary.

3. Cool and serve, refrigerate in an airtight container for up to 3 days, or transfer to an ice cube tray and freeze for up to 3 months.

BLF Tip: If you stop just before blending in step 2, your baby can explore soft table foods just like other family members can. Offer ingredients in ½-inch strips for easy pickup.

BABY GUACAMOLE

This fruit-filled dip (remember, avocado is a fruit) will not only be a tasty option the whole family will love, but its naturally soft texture, paired with its abundance of omega-3s, is the perfect option for your baby to safely enjoy. Plus, as your baby gets older and starts to explore more raw vegetables, it's a great dip option to help convince them to eat their veggies!

Makes 2 servings | **Serving size:** ¼ cup
Prep time: 5 minutes

GLUTEN-FREE, NUT-FREE, VEGETARIAN

1 small ripe avocado, halved and pitted

1 teaspoon minced fresh cilantro (optional)

1 tablespoon plain whole-milk yogurt

1 lime

1. Scoop out the avocado flesh and put it into a small bowl. Discard the avocado skins. Add the cilantro (if using) and yogurt to the avocado.

2. Using a fork or potato masher, smash and mix until a chunky puree texture is achieved.

3. Give the lime a quick roll on the countertop, then halve it and squeeze the juice of one half over the mixture (reserve the remaining half for another use). Stir, then serve with a spoon as a dip for veggies, spread on toast, or add a dollop to scrambled eggs.

BLF Tip: Spread a thin layer of guacamole on a strip of toast or pita bread or preload on a spoon for your baby to feed themselves. It's simple, allows you to eat your meal and model healthy habits, and lets them work on their motor skills.

SIMPLE SALMON WITH MASHED POTATOES

Salmon is a great option to offer to your baby, not only because of its soft texture, but also because fish contain many beneficial nutrients. Salmon in particular is one of the best sources of vitamin B$_{12}$ and also provides high levels of vitamin D and omega-3 fatty acids.

Makes 4 to 6 servings | **Serving size:** ¼ cup
Prep time: 10 minutes | **Cook time:** 15 minutes

GLUTEN-FREE, NUT-FREE

**2 medium yellow pota-
toes, peeled**

**3 tablespoons
unsalted butter**

**2 tablespoons whole-milk
Greek yogurt**

**Freshly ground black pepper
(optional)**

**½ cup flaked canned
salmon; bones removed**

1. Roughly cube the potatoes and put them into a small saucepan. Cover with water and bring to a boil over high heat. Cook until fork-tender, about 15 minutes. Remove from the heat.

2. Mash the hot potatoes with the butter and Greek yogurt until your desired consistency is reached. Season with pepper (if using).

3. Top the warm potatoes with the flaked salmon.

4. Serve immediately, refrigerate in an airtight container for up to 3 days, or transfer to an ice cube tray and freeze for up to 3 months.

Ingredient Tip: Using canned salmon without bones is convenient, but you can also prepare fresh or frozen salmon without the skin; just make sure to look for and remove any bones before serving it to your baby.

SWEETIE POTATO, APPLE, AND LENTIL PUREE

Potato, patahto, right? Not when it comes to actual potatoes. Each variety of potato, although all carbohydrate-rich, offers a unique nutrient profile. It's important that you offer your baby different varieties of potato. You often find sweet potatoes in baby food recipes and that's because of their amazing nutrient profile. Specifically, they contain fiber and antioxidants that promote optimal gut health.

Makes 4 to 6 servings | **Serving size:** ¼ cup
Prep time: 10 minutes | **Cook time:** 50 minutes

DAIRY-FREE, GLUTEN-FREE, NUT-FREE

- **1 cup water or low-sodium chicken or vegetable broth**
- **½ cup dry green, yellow, or red lentils, rinsed**
- **1 sweet potato, peeled and cut into chunks**
- **2 apples, peeled, cored, and cut into chunks**
- **¼ teaspoon cinnamon**

1. In a saucepan, bring the water to a boil and add the lentils.

2. Cover the pot and turn the heat down to let the lentils simmer for 30 to 40 minutes, until all the liquid is absorbed and the lentils are soft.

3. In another pot (or rice cooker), insert a steamer tray and add a little water.

4. Bring the water to a boil, then add the sweet potato and apples. Steam for 10 minutes, or until cooked through and soft.

5. Blend the lentils, sweet potato, apples, and cinnamon in a blender or food processor until smooth.

6. Serve immediately, refrigerate in an airtight container for up to 3 days, or transfer to an ice cube tray and freeze for up to 3 months.

Variation: Sweet potatoes are used quite often in baby food recipes. If you're looking for something different yet easy to swap, try using a hearty squash such as acorn or butternut.

TRIPLE PLAY HUMMUS

Hummus is a savory Middle Eastern dish that has quickly gained popularity across the globe. With its creamy texture, amazing nutrient profile, and versatility, it's a baby food trifecta. Hummus is traditionally made with tahini, which contains sesame seeds, a close contender to the top eight allergens. Hummus is a great way to safely offer sesame to your baby.

Makes 8 servings | **Serving size:** ¼ cup
Prep time: 10 minutes

DAIRY-FREE, GLUTEN-FREE, NUT-FREE, VEGAN

1 (15.5-ounce) can chickpeas, drained and rinsed

⅓ cup tahini

2 tablespoons lemon juice

2 or 3 garlic cloves

2 tablespoons olive oil

Pinch cumin

Pinch kosher salt

2 tablespoons seltzer

CLASSIC HUMMUS

1. Blend the chickpeas, tahini, lemon juice, garlic, olive oil, cumin, and salt in a food processor or blender. You may need to turn off the machine and scrape down the sides once or twice.

2. Blend to your desired consistency, adding the seltzer to help thin as needed. If you don't have seltzer, water or the liquid from the can of chickpeas works well.

3. Serve immediately, refrigerate in an airtight container for up to 4 days, or transfer to an ice cube tray and freeze for up to 4 months.

4 cups spinach, fresh
or frozen

¼ cup fresh basil, or
2 to 3 teaspoons frozen
basil, diced

6 ounces jarred roasted
red bell peppers (or
1 or 2 roasted red bell
peppers)

SPINACH PESTO HUMMUS

1. Make Classic Hummus, blending in the spinach and basil.

2. Serve immediately, refrigerate in an airtight container for up
to 4 days, or transfer to an ice cube tray and freeze for up to
4 months.

ROASTED RED PEPPER HUMMUS

1. Make Classic Hummus, blending in the roasted red bell
peppers.

2. Serve immediately, refrigerate in an airtight container for up
to 4 days, or transfer to an ice cube tray and freeze for up to
4 months.

BLF Tip: Hummus is great to spread on toast or a teething
cracker. It can even be offered as a dip to practice mastering
utensils and trying new foods.

69

CURRIED CAULIFLOWER AND CHICKPEAS

Baby food has often been pegged as bland, but yours doesn't have to be, especially when you make it yourself. You can and should use a variety of spices to flavor your baby's food. Adding spices such as curry powder to some of your favorite dishes helps your baby learn how to be an adventurous eater—something you'll be thankful for in the toddler years.

Makes 32 (1-ounce) freezer cubes | **Serving size:** ¼ cup (2 cubes)
Prep time: 5 minutes | **Cook time:** 10 minutes

DAIRY-FREE, GLUTEN-FREE, NUT-FREE, VEGAN

1 medium head fresh cauliflower, cored and coarsely chopped (about 1½ pounds)

1 (15.5-ounce) can low-sodium chickpeas, drained and rinsed

2 tablespoons olive oil

2 teaspoons mild curry powder

2 tablespoons water

1. In a medium saucepan with a steamer basket or insert, bring about 1 inch of water to a simmer. Add the cauliflower. Cover and simmer over low heat for 7 to 10 minutes, or until the cauliflower is soft.

2. In a blender or food processor, add the chickpeas, olive oil, curry powder, and water. Process until smooth.

3. Add the cooked cauliflower to the chickpea mixture. Blend until mostly smooth, adding a few additional tablespoons of water as needed to achieve your desired consistency.

4. Cool and serve, refrigerate in an airtight container for up to 3 days, or transfer to an ice cube tray and freeze for up to 3 months.

BLF Tip: Offer an extra-soft cooked cauliflower floret to your baby for easy self-feeding. Once your baby develops the pincer grasp, cooked, extra-soft chickpeas are the perfect size to easily pick up.

BEEF, BEANS, 'N' PRUNE PUREE

When you hear the word "constipated," your brain likely goes straight to prunes. This is because prunes contain a natural laxative called sorbitol. If you find that your baby has hard, pebble-like stools, adding "P" fruits such as prunes to recipes like this one can help things along their merry way. The "P" fruits include plums, peaches, pears, pineapple, and papaya.

Makes 4 servings | **Serving size:** ¼ cup
Prep time: 5 minutes | **Cook time:** 15 minutes

DAIRY-FREE, GLUTEN-FREE, NUT-FREE

1 cup trimmed green beans
½ pound ground beef
½ cup chopped prunes

1. Fill a medium saucepan with about 1 inch of water and bring to a simmer. Place the green beans in a steamer basket, set it over the simmering water, cover, and cook until tender, about 8 minutes. Allow to cool.

2. While the green beans are steaming, cook the ground beef over medium-low heat in a medium sauté pan or skillet, stirring frequently and breaking the beef into small pieces with a spoon as it browns, for about 15 minutes, until browned evenly and cooked through.

3. Drain the excess fat from the pan and allow the beef to cool.

4. In a blender or food processor, puree the cooled beef and green beans along with the prunes until your desired consistency is reached. Add water if necessary.

5. Serve immediately, refrigerate in an airtight container for up to 3 days, or transfer to an ice cube tray and freeze for up to 3 months.

BLF Tip: Try placing an extra-soft, cooked whole green bean on your baby's tray and let them explore feeding themselves.

HAPPY BELLY SMOOTHIE

It's always good to have a remedy for constipation, now that your baby has started solids. This smoothie will do just what its name says: keep foods moving along, leaving your baby's belly happy and not backed up. Dates, flaxseed, and a combination of "P" fruits are the perfect combination to ease your baby's backups.

Makes 6 to 8 servings | **Serving size:** ¼ cup
Prep time: 5 minutes

DAIRY-FREE, GLUTEN-FREE, VEGETARIAN

½ cup frozen peaches

2 Medjool dates, pitted

2 prunes

1 cup almond milk

1 tablespoon ground
flaxseed

½ teaspoon cinnamon
(optional)

1. Combine the peaches, dates, prunes, almond milk, flaxseed, and cinnamon (if using) in a blender and process until smooth, about 1 minute.

2. Serve immediately or transfer to empty ice pop molds and freeze for up to 3 months.

BLF Tip: You can offer this recipe as a traditional puree or in a straw cup for practice mastering a straw. If you're feeling extra adventurous and it's bath night, offer a small amount in an open cup.

CREAMY TOMATO SOUP

This recipe is a great upgrade from the traditional canned tomato soup that's too high in sodium for your baby. It contains blended chickpeas that help make it an easy texture for your baby to work with; low-sodium canned tomatoes for a kick of vitamin C; and delicious herbs and spices for a unique flavor.

Makes 16 servings | **Serving size:** ¼ cup
Prep time: 5 minutes | **Cook time:** 25 minutes

DAIRY-FREE, GLUTEN-FREE, NUT-FREE, VEGAN

2 tablespoons extra-virgin olive oil

1 small onion, diced

4 garlic cloves, diced

1 (28-ounce) can low-sodium diced or crushed tomatoes

½ cup low-sodium vegetable stock

1½ cups canned chickpeas, drained and rinsed

½ teaspoon oregano

Course salt

1. In a stockpot or Dutch oven over medium heat, heat the olive oil until it shimmers. Add the diced onion and cook, stirring occasionally, until softened. Add the garlic and cook, stirring frequently for 1 to 2 minutes, or until fragrant.

2. Pour in the tomatoes (without draining) and vegetable stock. Stir in the chickpeas. Sprinkle in the oregano, cover, and let simmer for about 15 minutes.

3. Blend the soup with an immersion blender until smooth, or in batches in a food processor.

4. Let cool to a warm temperature, and top with coarse salt before serving.

5. Refrigerate leftovers in an airtight container for up to 3 days, or transfer to an ice cube tray and freeze for up to 3 months.

BLF Tip: Dips are great to help promote self-feeding. Offer this recipe in a suction bowl to decrease spillage and pair with toast or Parmesan Zucchini Cakes (page 84) for dipping.

Mini Quinoa-Turkey Meatballs

Page 77

Chapter Five

First Finger Foods
(8–10 Months and Up)

BANANA-AVOCADO FREEZY POPS

Bananas, avocado, and popsicles: what's not to love? (Especially for a teething baby.) You may find that at some point your baby starts to turn their nose up at every food you offer. This may be due to teething, which can make it uncomfortable to munch on anything. Try not to take it personally. This is when you whip out these nutrient-rich popsicles.

Makes 6 small ice pops | **Serving size:** 1 ice pop
Prep time: 10 minutes, plus 6+ hours freezing time

GLUTEN-FREE, NUT-FREE, VEGETARIAN

1 very ripe banana

1 ripe avocado

½ cup plain whole-milk Greek yogurt

1. Combine the banana, avocado, and yogurt in a food processor and blend until smooth and creamy.

2. Using a rubber spatula, scoop the mixture out of the blender into ice pop molds or small paper cups. If using paper cups, cover each cup with tin foil and press a baby spoon or self-feeding utensil through the foil into the mixture.

3. Freeze until solid, about 6 hours or overnight. If using paper cups, peel off the paper cup and remove the foil once frozen.

4. Store in the freezer for up to 3 months.

Good to Know: Popsicle molds are a must-have kitchen tool when introducing solids, but it's important to get a version that's easy for your baby to hold. Check out the Resources on page 122 for recommendations on popsicle molds.

MINI QUINOA-TURKEY MEATBALLS

This healthy spin on homemade meatballs is the perfect combination of nutrients and flavor. With three different sources of protein and iron—turkey, eggs, and quinoa—plus tomato paste to aid iron absorption, you can feel great offering these to your baby. You can easily swap ground beef for the turkey and quick oats for the quinoa if you're looking for a change.

Makes 24 meatballs | **Serving size:** 2 meatballs
Prep time: 10 minutes | **Cook time:** 30 minutes

DAIRY-FREE, NUT-FREE

1 pound ground turkey

2 cups cooked quinoa

1 apple, peeled and grated

2 large eggs, lightly beaten

2 tablespoons tomato paste

1 teaspoon chopped fresh or dried basil

1 teaspoon garlic powder

1 teaspoon dried oregano

3 tablespoons extra-virgin olive oil

1. Preheat the oven to 350°F. Line a rimmed baking sheet with parchment paper.

2. In a large bowl, combine the turkey, quinoa, apple, eggs, tomato paste, basil, garlic powder, and oregano until well mixed. Use a 1-tablespoon measuring spoon to scoop the mixture and roll each scoop into a mini meatball. Place each meatball a few inches apart on the prepared baking sheet.

3. Drizzle the meatballs with the olive oil and bake for about 30 minutes, or until they reach an interior temperature of at least 165°F. Let rest for a few minutes.

4. Serve immediately, refrigerate in an airtight container for up to 3 days, or freeze for up to 3 months. To cook, place frozen meatballs on a prepared baking sheet (do not thaw), and follow step 3, adding about 15 minutes to the cooking time.

BLF Tip: As they learn to pick up foods with their pointer finger and thumb (pincer grasp), you can start chopping up the meatballs into pea-size pieces.

BANANA BREAD BITES

Use this recipe to get rid of those brown bananas that have been sitting in your freezer for far too long. One of the best features of this recipe is that you can offer your baby a sweet, muffin-like option without the added sugar. This is a recipe you'll be making again and again because your baby will love it so much and it's so easy to whip up.

Makes 24 muffins | **Serving size:** 2 muffins
Prep time: 5 minutes | **Cook time:** 10 to 15 minutes

VEGETARIAN

Unsalted butter, for greasing the pan

1 large, very ripe banana (1 cup mashed)

½ cup milk

2 teaspoons apple cider vinegar

2 teaspoons vanilla extract

3 tablespoons coconut oil, melted

¾ cup unbleached all-purpose flour

½ teaspoon baking powder

½ teaspoon baking soda

½ teaspoon cinnamon

1. Preheat the oven to 350°F. Butter a mini muffin tin.

2. In a large bowl, mash the banana with the milk. Stir in the vinegar, vanilla, and melted coconut oil and mix until well combined.

3. Add the flour, baking powder, baking soda, and cinnamon and mix until combined.

4. Pour into the greased mini muffin tin and bake for 10 to 15 minutes, or until the tops spring back when touched.

5. Serve immediately, refrigerate in an airtight container for up to 3 days, or freeze for up to 3 months.

Ingredient Tip: Instead of tossing your bananas with the peel on into the freezer, peel them, place them on a baking sheet to freeze, then combine them in a freezer bag once frozen.

ONE-PAN LENTIL DAL

Dal is an intensely spiced dish made with pulses, in this case lentils. It's essentially a thick puree of lentils and spices that will expose your baby to a wide variety of flavors, something you know I've mentioned is important. If you're short on time, look in the rice and beans aisle of your grocery store for a steamer lentil packet you can quickly prepare in the microwave.

Makes 24 servings | **Serving size:** ¼ cup
Prep time: 10 minutes | **Cook time:** 25 minutes

DAIRY-FREE, GLUTEN-FREE, VEGAN

- **2 tablespoons coconut oil**
- **1 onion, diced**
- **2 large carrots, diced**
- **4 garlic cloves, minced**
- **1 tablespoon finely chopped ginger root**
- **1 teaspoon curry powder**
- **½ teaspoon cumin**
- **¼ teaspoon salt**
- **1 (28-ounce) can low-sodium diced tomatoes**
- **1 cup low-sodium vegetable broth or water**
- **1 can full-fat coconut milk**
- **1 cup red lentils, rinsed**

1. In a large skillet over medium heat, melt the coconut oil. Add the onion, carrots, garlic, and ginger. Cook until the vegetables start to soften. Stir in the curry powder, cumin, and salt and cook for 1 to 2 minutes more.

2. Pour in the tomatoes, broth, and coconut milk, then add the lentils. Bring to a simmer, stirring occasionally. Cover and reduce the heat to medium-low. Cook, still stirring occasionally, until the lentils are tender, about 20 minutes.

3. Serve immediately, refrigerate in an airtight container for up to 3 days, or transfer to an ice cube tray and freeze for up to 2 months.

Good to Know: Coconuts are technically considered a tree nut, therefore are a part of the top eight common allergens. If your baby has a tree nut allergy, you can substitute olive oil. Substitute cow's milk or a milk of choice for the coconut milk. Always speak with your baby's pediatrician regarding food allergies.
Pairing Tip: Serve this alongside Ginger Poached Chicken (page 85).

EGG-CELLENT ASPARAGUS FRITTATAS

Eggs are one of the best table foods to offer your baby. Not only do they have a manageable texture, but research now suggests that introducing eggs early and often can help decrease the risk of food allergies. You can easily offer eggs in a variety of ways to ensure your baby gets a solid dose of choline, lutein, protein, fat, and a variety of vitamins and minerals.

Makes 12 mini-muffin frittatas | **Serving size:** 2 muffins
Prep time: 5 minutes | **Cook time:** 15 minutes

GLUTEN-FREE, NUT-FREE, VEGETARIAN

1 teaspoon olive oil

3 large eggs

2 tablespoons grated cheddar cheese

¼ cup diced asparagus

1. Preheat the oven to 375°F. Grease 12 wells of a mini-muffin tin with the olive oil.

2. Crack the eggs into a medium bowl and whisk. Whisk in the cheese. Add the asparagus and stir.

3. Pour the mixture into the muffin cups until each is about two-thirds full.

4. Bake for 12 to 14 minutes.

5. Cut each frittata into smaller pieces before serving.

6. Serve immediately, refrigerate in an airtight container for up to 3 days, or freeze for up to 3 months.

BLF Tip: Try offering ½-inch strips of frittata to your baby as one of their first foods. Eggs have a soft texture that is safe to offer from the get-go.

CHEESY TURKEY QUESADILLAS

Quesadillas are a great way to jam-pack one dish with a bunch of nutrients. When I need to make a quick dinner, I love to whip up quesadillas and throw in leftovers or produce that's nearing its final hours. My kids love quesadillas because they enjoy having something to dip and dunk. Try plain Greek yogurt instead of sour cream for more protein.

Makes 2 servings | **Serving size:** ½ quesadilla
Prep time: 5 minutes | **Cook time:** 5 minutes

NUT-FREE

2 slices turkey breast meat

2 corn tortillas

¼ cup shredded ched-dar cheese

1. Layer the turkey on one of the tortillas and sprinkle with the cheese. Place the other tortilla over it to cover.

2. In a medium sauté pan or skillet, cook the quesadilla over medium heat until the cheese has melted, about 2 minutes on each side.

3. Allow the quesadilla to cool a little, then cut into bite-size pieces.

4. Serve immediately, refrigerate in an airtight container for up to 3 days, or freeze for up to 3 months (the quality will deteriorate the longer they are frozen).

Preparation Tip: For a speedier option and without using the stovetop, simply throw the quesadilla with all the ingredients into the microwave and cook until the cheese is melted. Fold and voila! A quick and easy dinner without using a pan.

SPEEDY PASTA PRIMAVERA

This healthy pasta recipe comes together quickly and provides your baby with a balanced meal of whole grains and a variety of vegetables that the whole family can enjoy. Research suggests that people who eat together as a family three or more times per week are likely to be a healthier weight and make healthier food choices. Set your baby up for future success.

Makes 8 servings | **Serving size:** ¼ cup
Prep time: 5 minutes | **Cook time:** 10 minutes

NUT-FREE, VEGETARIAN

3 cups water

1 cup whole-wheat fusilli

1 tablespoon olive oil

½ cup shredded zucchini

½ cup shredded carrots

½ cup chopped asparagus

1 tablespoon unsalted butter

2 tablespoons grated Parmesan cheese

1. In a large pot, bring the water to a boil over high heat. Add the pasta and reduce the heat to medium. Cook until the pasta is tender, about 10 minutes. Drain the pasta in a colander, reserving ¼ cup of the cooking water.

2. While the pasta is cooking, in a medium sauté pan or skillet, heat the olive oil over medium-high heat. Add the zucchini, carrot, and asparagus, and sauté until soft, about 8 minutes.

3. Transfer the vegetables to a large bowl. Combine the pasta, reserved pasta cooking water, zucchini, carrots, asparagus, butter, and Parmesan and toss.

4. Serve immediately, refrigerate in an airtight container for up to 3 days, or freeze for up to 3 months.

Variation: If you need a wheat- or gluten-free option, try a lentil-based pasta. This pasta will have even more vitamins and minerals, specifically iron.

MINI BAKED RICE BALLS

You may find that your baby starts to love anything carbohydrate-filled. This is common and completely normal. Carbohydrates are our body's main source of energy and almost all foods contain some form of carbs. When it comes to preparing carbohydrate-rich grains such as rice, I love the quick and easy frozen rice steamers, which are great for saving on time and dirty dishes.

Makes 20 rice balls | **Serving size:** 2 rice balls
Prep time: 10 minutes | **Cook time:** 20 minutes

NUT-FREE, VEGETARIAN

- **¼ cup whole-wheat pastry flour**
- **2 large eggs, beaten**
- **½ cup bread crumbs**
- **1 cup cooked brown rice**
- **⅓ cup shredded mozzarella cheese**
- **¼ cup chopped spinach**

1. Preheat the oven to 375°F. Line a 9-by-13-inch baking sheet with parchment paper.

2. Place the flour, beaten eggs, and bread crumbs in three separate small bowls.

3. In a medium bowl, combine the rice, cheese, and spinach.

4. Scoop up about 1 tablespoon of the rice mixture and roll it into a ball using your hands. Roll the ball in the flour, then dip it in the egg, and then roll it in the bread crumbs. Place the ball on the prepared baking sheet. Repeat with the remaining rice mixture.

5. Bake for 5 to 8 minutes; turn over and bake for 5 to 8 minutes more.

6. Serve immediately, refrigerate in an airtight container for up to 3 days, or freeze for up to 3 months.

Pairing Tip: Offer with Creamy Tomato Soup (page 73) for a fun dip and boost of vitamin C.

PARMESAN ZUCCHINI CAKES

Any time you can add vegetables to a kid-favorite dish is a bonus. As your baby starts to get older and more particular, try not to "hide" veggies, but rather have your baby help you add them. Hiding can lead to distrust at meals, something that will not work to your advantage. Feel free to also change up the size of these pancakes and make veggie tots.

Makes 24 pancakes | **Serving size:** 2 pancakes
Prep time: 10 minutes | **Cook time:** 25 minutes

NUT-FREE, VEGETARIAN

1 tablespoon olive oil

3 medium zucchinis (about 1 pound), grated and squeezed to remove excess liquid

2 large eggs

½ teaspoon garlic powder

½ teaspoon onion powder

Freshly ground black pepper

¼ cup grated Parmesan cheese

½ cup whole wheat flour

1. Preheat the oven to 400°F. Drizzle the olive oil onto a rimmed baking sheet.

2. In a medium bowl, combine the zucchini, eggs, garlic powder, onion powder, black pepper, and Parmesan cheese. Mix until well combined. Add the flour and mix until combined.

3. For each pancake, spoon 2 tablespoons of pancake mixture onto the prepared baking sheet. Bake for 20 to 25 minutes, flipping halfway, until both sides are golden brown.

4. Remove from the oven and cool on a wire rack.

5. Serve immediately, refrigerate in an airtight container for up to 3 days, or freeze flat on a baking sheet then transfer to a freezer bag for up to 3 months. Reheat the pancakes from frozen; there is no need to defrost. Place on a baking sheet in a 350°F oven for about 10 minutes, or until heated through. Allow to cool before serving.

Preparation Tip: Zucchinis are 95-percent water. To prevent a soggy pancake, make sure to squeeze the grated zucchini extra well.

GINGER POACHED CHICKEN

Don't be scared by the word "poaching." This cooking technique may not be a part of your everyday routine, but it's great for making an ultra-moist product. Poaching simply means to cook in a small amount of liquid. When offering your baby soft table foods, moist proteins are key to make it easier to mash in their mouth and decrease the risk of choking. The ginger not only offers immune benefits, but an extra boost of flavor.

Makes 20 servings | **Serving size:** ¼ cup
Prep time: 5 minutes | **Cook time:** 45 minutes

DAIRY-FREE, GLUTEN-FREE, NUT-FREE

2 bone-in, skin-on chicken breasts (about 2 pounds)

2 scallions, trimmed

1 (2-inch) piece ginger, peeled and thinly sliced

1. In a large saucepot, place the chicken, scallions, and ginger. Cover with cool water.

2. Heat the pot over medium heat until barely simmering. Reduce the heat to low to maintain a simmer. Partially cover and cook for 30 to 45 minutes, or until the chicken registers 160°F when a thermometer is inserted into the thickest part of the breast.

3. Transfer the chicken from the cooking liquid to a plate and allow to cool, saving the cooking liquid for another use. When the chicken is cool enough to handle, remove the skin and bones, and cut the meat into pea-size pieces.

4. Serve immediately, refrigerate in an airtight container for up to 3 days, or freeze for up to 3 months.

Pairing Tip: This dish pairs well with One-Pan Lentil Dal (page 79) or Sweetie Potato, Apple, and Lentil Puree (page 66).

FIRST FINGER FOODS (8–10 MONTHS AND UP)

BAKED SWEET POTATO FRIES

Making homemade fries is an easy way to enjoy a fast-food favorite in a healthier way. Most fries are deep-fried in oil, whereas this recipe opts for baking with olive oil, a heart-healthy fat that's great for brain development. Feel free to leave the skin on the fries for extra fiber, making them an even healthier option for your baby.

Makes 4 to 6 servings | **Serving size:** ¼ cup
Prep time: 10 minutes | **Cook time:** 20 minutes

GLUTEN-FREE, NUT-FREE, VEGAN OPTION

2 tablespoons olive oil or melted unsalted butter, plus more for greasing

2 pounds sweet potatoes

1 tablespoon cornstarch (optional)

½ teaspoon kosher salt

Pinch cinnamon

1. Preheat the oven to 425°F.

2. Prepare a baking sheet by lightly coating it with olive oil.

3. Wash and scrub the sweet potatoes. Scrub them thoroughly if you're keeping the skin.

4. Cut the potatoes into sticks, about ¼-inch wide and ¼-inch thick.

5. Place the fries into a large bowl or plastic bag.

6. If using cornstarch, toss the fries in cornstarch and salt, then spread them out on the prepared baking sheet in a single layer. Drizzle with the olive oil, then sprinkle with the cinnamon.

7. Bake for roughly 10 minutes, or until light brown and crispy, then flip and bake for an additional 10 minutes.

8. Serve immediately.

Good to Know: Getting your kids involved in the kitchen as early as possible will help decrease mealtime battles in the future. Feel free to switch up the seasonings and even have your baby help sprinkle them on.

Preparation Tip: After cutting the sweet potatoes, prepare the amount you want for one meal, then store the rest in a freezer bag in the freezer for up to 3 months. Any time you can save a few minutes of slicing and dicing is a huge help when you're trying to get dinner on the table quickly.

YOGURT-COVERED BLUEBERRY KABOBS

Throw some blueberries on a stick, roll them in some yogurt, and BAM—you have instant interest from your baby and a nutrient-dense snack for them. I like to use the coffee stoppers you get when you purchase a fancy coffee. It's a great way to reuse and reduce plastic waste, and they tend to have a rounded edge for safety. There you go: the perfect excuse to run and grab a coffee.

Makes 3 skewers | **Serving size:** 1 skewer
Prep time: 15 minutes | **Cook time:** 5 minutes

GLUTEN-FREE, NUT-FREE, VEGAN OPTION

1 pint fresh blueberries

1 cup plain full-fat Greek yogurt (or yogurt alternative for vegan option)

1. Prepare a baking sheet by lining it with parchment paper, foil, or wax paper.

2. Wash the blueberries carefully, showing your child how the berries "take a bath," then pat them dry.

3. Thread some blueberries onto your chosen stick, then roll in the yogurt.

4. Lay the skewers in a single layer on the prepared baking sheet, then freeze for at least 1 hour until the yogurt has hardened. They will keep in the freezer for up to 3 months.

5. Let thaw for about 5 minutes before enjoying.

Variation: Prior to rolling the blueberries in yogurt, mix a little nut butter into the yogurt for a boost of heart-healthy fats and exposure to common allergens.

BAKED TOFU WITH SESAME DIPPING SAUCE

Maybe you're wondering, "What the heck is in tofu anyways?" Tofu is essentially pressed soy milk. Its nutrient profile is pretty impressive, and tofu is an extremely nutrient-dense food. Even if you aren't vegetarian or vegan, tofu is a great option to add to your baby's diet. Plus, it helps introduce soy, which is one of the top eight allergens, in a safe and easy way.

Makes 6 to 8 servings | **Serving size:** ¼ cup
Prep time: 1 hour | **Cook time:** 20 minutes

DAIRY-FREE, GLUTEN-FREE OPTION, NUT-FREE, VEGAN

1 tablespoon olive oil

3 tablespoons maple syrup

1 tablespoon sesame oil

2 tablespoons soy sauce (or tamari for gluten-free option)

2 garlic cloves, diced

¼ teaspoon ground ginger, or ½ teaspoon grated fresh ginger

1 block firm tofu, pressed and cubed

1. Preheat the oven to 425°F.

2. Prepare a baking sheet by lining it with foil and lightly coating it with the olive oil.

3. In a small bowl, mix the maple syrup, sesame oil, soy sauce, garlic, and ginger together. Marinate the tofu in half of the sauce and reserve the rest for dipping.

4. Lay out the tofu on the prepared baking sheet and bake for 10 minutes on each side.

5. Cool and serve, refrigerate in an airtight container for up to 3 days, or freeze for up to 3 months.

Good to Know: Make sure not to substitute honey for maple syrup. Honey should not be offered until your baby is 12 months of age to avoid infant botulism.

TWO-INGREDIENT PANCAKES

Yes, you really can make pancakes from only two ingredients: egg and banana. The moist consistency of these pancakes paired with the easy-to-hold shape makes them a safe option for your baby to enjoy. And with the natural sweetness from the banana, there's no need for any maple syrup. Go on, try these!

Makes 6 to 8 (2-inch) pancakes | **Serving size:** 1 pancake
Prep time: 5 minutes | **Cook time:** 5 minutes

GLUTEN-FREE, NUT-FREE, VEGETARIAN

1 ripe banana

2 large eggs, lightly beaten

1 tablespoon unsalted butter, for greasing the pan

1. In a medium bowl, mash the banana until it has a pudding-like consistency.

2. Stir in the eggs until completely incorporated.

3. Heat a medium skillet over medium heat. Put the butter into the pan, and when it begins to sizzle, drop about 2 tablespoons of batter on the hot skillet for each pancake. (The batter should begin to sizzle immediately.) Repeat until the pan is filled, leaving 1 to 2 inches between each pancake.

4. Cook for about 1 minute. The corners should be set, and when you peek at the underside, it should be golden brown. Carefully flip the pancakes and cook for about 1 minute more, or until browned.

5. Serve warm with toppings of your choice, like butter, peanut butter, or maple syrup.

6. Serve immediately, refrigerate in an airtight container for up to 3 days, or freeze for up to 3 months.

Variation: Add a pinch of cinnamon to introduce a new flavor.

90

BAKED SALMON FISH STICKS

Store-bought fish sticks, although tasty, tend to be a bit higher in sodium than is ideal for babies. This homemade version using salmon is easy, delicious, and will offer up more omega-3s for your baby's optimal brain development. The more you can control the ingredients in the food you serve your family, the better, but know that it's also okay to incorporate convenience for the sake of your sanity and time.

Makes 4 to 6 servings | **Serving size:** 1 fish stick
Prep time: 15 minutes | **Cook time:** 20 minutes

DAIRY-FREE, NUT-FREE

1½ pounds frozen skinless salmon, thawed and patted dry

1 large egg

2 cups panko bread crumbs

¼ teaspoon sea salt

¼ teaspoon freshly ground black pepper

¼ cup olive oil

1. Preheat the oven to 400°F. Line a rimmed baking sheet with parchment paper.

2. Cut the salmon into 1- to 1½-inch-thick strips.

3. Gather 2 small bowls. In the first bowl, lightly beat the egg. In the second bowl, combine the panko bread crumbs, salt, and pepper.

4. Set up an assembly line: One by one, dip the salmon strips in the egg, and then roll them in the bread crumbs, coating the fish evenly and thoroughly. Gently tap off any excess breading and place the fish sticks on the prepared baking sheet.

5. Drizzle the olive oil over the fish sticks and use your clean hands to roll the fish sticks around to ensure all the breading is coated with oil.

6. Bake for 15 to 20 minutes, flipping halfway through, until the fish sticks are lightly browned on all sides.

7. Serve immediately, refrigerate in an airtight container for up to 3 days, or freeze for up to 3 months.

FIRST FINGER FOODS (8–10 MONTHS AND UP)

ALMOND BUTTERY GREEN BEANS

Green beans are great to turn to for a quick and easy side dish. This recipe gives you a way to change up the flavor, provide a boost of healthy fats, and introduce variety, all at the same time. Any time I can add a nut butter to recipes is a plus; my kids will eat it and it's a healthy calorie boost for them.

Makes 16 servings | **Serving size:** ¼ cup
Prep time: 5 minutes | **Cook time:** 15 minutes

DAIRY-FREE, GLUTEN-FREE, VEGETARIAN

½ cup creamy unsalted almond butter

¼ cup lemon juice

¼ cup olive oil

4 cups fresh or frozen green beans

1. In a small bowl, combine the almond butter, lemon juice, and olive oil. Set aside, or refrigerate or freeze the sauce to use later.

2. In a medium saucepan with a steamer basket or insert, bring about 1 inch of water to a simmer. Add the green beans. Cover and simmer over low heat for 10 to 15 minutes, until the green beans are soft.

3. Allow the green beans to cool slightly and cut into pieces about the size of a pea. Toss ¼ cup green beans with 1 tablespoon of the sauce, or serve the sauce on the side as a dip.

4. Serve immediately or refrigerate in an airtight container for up to 3 days.

Pairing Tip: This green bean dish works well with Chicken Parm Pasta Bake (page 108) or Ginger Poached Chicken (page 85).
Variation: Toss the almond butter sauce with other veggies, such as cauliflower, carrots, or asparagus.

Smashed-
Bean
Quesadillas
with Easy
Salsa Dip
Page 106

Chapter Six

Advanced Finger Foods
(12 Months and Up)

CHICKEN AND VEGGIE BAKED RICE

This one-pot dish not only saves you time washing dishes, but it can also help you use up any produce lurking in your refrigerator. One of the beautiful things about cooking is that you can be creative. Feel free to veer from this recipe and add different veggies, herbs, and spices to make it your own.

Makes 10 to 12 servings | **Serving size:** ¼ cup
Prep time: 15 minutes | **Cook time:** 55 minutes

DAIRY-FREE, GLUTEN-FREE, NUT-FREE

- **4 tablespoons extra-virgin olive oil, divided**
- **1 whole chicken breast, diced**
- **¼ teaspoon sea salt, divided**
- **1 large sweet onion, chopped**
- **1⅓ cups brown rice**
- **8 ounces snap peas, trimmed and cut into pieces**
- **2 carrots, peeled and cut into small pieces**

1. Preheat the oven to 400°F.

2. In a Dutch oven or large oven-safe skillet over medium heat, warm 2 tablespoons olive oil. Add the chicken and ⅛ teaspoon salt and brown on each side for 3 minutes. Transfer the chicken to a plate and set aside.

3. Add the remaining 2 tablespoons olive oil and the onion to the Dutch oven and cook for 4 minutes. Add the rice, snap peas, carrots, broccoli, and mushrooms and sauté for 2 minutes. Add the chicken broth, curry powder, and the remaining ⅛ teaspoon salt, stir well, and bring to a simmer.

4. Cover with a lid and bake for 30 minutes.

5. Add the chicken and continue to bake for an additional 15 minutes, or until the rice is cooked.

½ head broccoli, cut into
   florets, chopped, and
   stems discarded

1 cup chopped cremini
   mushrooms

4 cups low-sodium
   chicken broth

1 tablespoon curry powder

6. Serve immediately or refrigerate in an airtight container for up to 3 days.

Good to Know: When frozen and thawed, rice is often mushy and loses quality. Therefore I don't recommend freezing this recipe.
Variation: Want to make this vegetarian or vegan? Skip straight to step 3 and add a side of beans or the baked tofu from page 89.

97

CHEESY TOMATO CORN MUFFINS

This recipe is a brilliant combination of cheesy goodness and sweet cherry tomatoes wrapped in a fun-size muffin. The best thing about this recipe, besides the fact that it's a healthy muffin, is that you can switch up the vegetable ingredients. If you don't have cherry tomatoes, try broccoli or asparagus. Make a double batch, store in the freezer, and pull some out when you need a quick snack or easy side dish.

Makes 12 (1-muffin) servings or 24 (2-mini-muffin) servings | **Serving size:** 1 muffin or 2 mini-muffins
Prep time: 5 minutes | **Cook time:** 25 minutes

NUT-FREE, VEGETARIAN

⅔ cup cornmeal

⅔ cup all-purpose flour

1 teaspoon baking powder

½ teaspoon baking soda

¼ teaspoon salt

½ cup extra-virgin olive oil

½ cup whole milk

2 medium eggs

1 cup grated cheddar cheese

1 cup halved cherry tomatoes

⅔ cup canned corn, rinsed and drained

1. Preheat the oven to 400°F. Line a 12-cup muffin tin with paper or silicone liners.

2. In a large bowl, gently whisk together the cornmeal, flour, baking powder, baking soda, and salt. Mix in the olive oil, milk, and eggs until well combined.

3. Add the cheese and mix until well combined. Add the tomatoes and corn and mix well.

4. Fill the muffin cups about two-thirds full. Bake for 20 to 25 minutes. Let the muffins cool for 10 minutes before enjoying warm.

5. Serve immediately, refrigerate in an airtight container for up to 3 days, or freeze for up to 3 months.

Good to Know: You can also try a mini muffin pan to yield smaller muffins. Prepare as above and bake for roughly half the time.
Ingredient Tip: Try using frozen corn instead of canned.

BUTTERNUT SQUASH RISOTTO

Risotto alone is a delicious side dish, but add some butternut squash and you have a sweet and savory dish with a rock star lineup: vitamins A, C, E, and basically all the Bs, plus a bunch of great nutrition players on the bench. Once you try butternut squash in this recipe, you'll want to start adding it to other amazing grain dishes, such as classic macaroni and cheese.

Makes 16 servings | **Serving size:** ¼ cup
Prep time: 10 minutes | **Cook time:** 1 hour 15 minutes + 45 minutes cooling time

GLUTEN-FREE, NUT-FREE, VEGETARIAN

1 medium butternut squash

2 tablespoons extra-virgin olive oil

½ teaspoon salt, plus more to taste

Freshly ground black pepper

8 cups low-sodium vegetable broth, divided

1. Preheat the oven to 400°F. Line a rimmed baking sheet with parchment paper.

2. Carefully cut the squash in half lengthwise. Scoop out the seeds with a spoon or ice cream scoop. Gently score the squash with a knife, drizzle with olive oil, and season with the salt and pepper. Place the squash on the prepared baking sheet and roast for 45 to 60 minutes, until it is fork-tender in the thickest part of the squash. Let cool 30 to 45 minutes.

3. Scoop the cooled squash flesh from the skin into a large bowl. Use a handheld mixer to blend the squash with 2 cups vegetable broth until smooth. Set aside.

4. In a medium pot over low heat or in a glass bowl in a microwave, heat the remaining 6 cups vegetable broth. Keep warm.

continued

3 tablespoons
   unsalted butter

1 medium onion, diced

1½ cups Arborio rice

⅛ teaspoon turmeric

¼ cup heavy
   (whipping) cream

½ cup grated or shaved
   Parmesan cheese, plus
   more for garnish

Minced parsley, for garnish

100

5. In a large pot over medium heat, melt the butter. Add the onions and cook until translucent, 2 to 3 minutes. Add the Arborio rice and stir, cooking for 1 minute. Reduce the heat to low. In 1-cup increments, add the warmed vegetable broth to the skillet, stirring continuously while the broth is slowly absorbed. Continue until all 6 cups have been added and the rice starts to become tender. Season with salt and pepper and taste for desired tenderness.

6. When the rice is done, gently stir in the semi-pureed squash and season with the turmeric. Pour in the heavy cream and add the cheese, stirring until just combined. Taste and add more salt and pepper as needed. Sprinkle parsley over the top.

7. Serve immediately, refrigerate in an airtight container for up to 3 days, or freeze for up to 3 months.

Ingredient Tip: If you can't find Arborio rice, substitute pearled barley, orzo, or jasmine rice. To save on time, purchase peeled, precut butternut squash or frozen butternut squash and skip the roasting.

SIMPLE SPINACH PESTO PASTA

Traditionally, pesto is made with pine nuts, which can be rather expensive. The good news is that you can get a similar flavor in this pasta dish without the pine nuts. This recipe is safe for children with tree nut allergies, but if you want the real deal, purchase premade pesto and skip straight to step 4.

Makes 4 servings | **Serving size:** ¼ cup
Prep time: 5 minutes | **Cook time:** 10 minutes

NUT-FREE, VEGETARIAN

3 cups water

1 cup small-shape whole-wheat pasta (such as ditalini or elbow macaroni)

2 cups baby spinach

1 cup chopped fresh basil

½ tablespoon freshly squeezed lemon juice

2 tablespoons grated Parmesan cheese

¼ cup olive oil

1. In a medium pot, bring the water to a boil over high heat.

2. Add the pasta and reduce the heat to medium. Cook until the pasta is tender, 5 to 8 minutes. Drain the pasta in a colander.

3. In a blender or food processor, combine the spinach, basil, lemon juice, Parmesan, and olive oil and puree until smooth.

4. In a large bowl, combine the pasta and pesto.

5. Serve immediately, refrigerate in an airtight container for up to 3 days, or freeze for up to 3 months.

Preparation Tip: If you know you will be freezing this dish for later, try cooking the noodles a bit less, so when you reheat them they won't be mushy.
Variation: Each time you make this simple recipe, switch up the shape of the pasta. Even though it's still pasta, it exposes your baby to a different variety, helping them be a more adventurous eater.

BEEF AND BROCCOLI TREES

I love Chinese takeout but the dishes are often loaded with sodium, which is not the best choice for your baby. It's not that you can't ever enjoy Chinese takeout again; but try to eat a healthier homemade alternative more often than takeout. Plus, this recipe is quicker than waiting for delivery. Throw a bag of frozen broccoli in the microwave to make preparation even speedier.

Makes 4 servings | **Serving size:** ¼ cup
Prep time: 5 minutes | **Cook time:** 15 minutes

DAIRY-FREE, NUT-FREE

1 tablespoon olive oil

¾ pound filet of beef, cut into bite-size pieces

1 cup broccoli florets

½ cup water

1 tablespoon low-sodium soy sauce (optional)

1 teaspoon sesame oil

1. In a large skillet, heat the olive oil over medium heat. Add the beef and cook, stirring occasionally, until browned, about 4 minutes. Transfer to a plate using a slotted spoon.

2. Add the broccoli and water to the pan and cook until the broccoli is tender and the liquid has evaporated, 5 to 8 minutes.

3. Return the beef and any collected juices to the pan and cook, stirring, until the beef is warmed through, about 1 minute.

4. Remove from the heat. Add the soy sauce, if using, and the sesame oil.

5. Serve immediately, refrigerate in an airtight container for up to 3 days, or freeze for up to 3 months.

Pairing Tip: Serve alongside brown rice or noodles to make the meal feel more complete.

102

POLENTA PIZZA SQUARES

If you ask me, every Friday night should be pizza night. But eating the same type of pizza can get boring and too high in sodium, especially for your toddler. Try switching it up with a simple recipe like this one. Use pizza nights as a way to enjoy vegetable toppings on a beloved favorite. Switching the crust to polenta provides great exposure to different flavors and more complex carbohydrates than traditional crust may provide.

Makes 4 to 6 servings | **Serving size:** 1 square
Prep time: 15 minutes | **Cook time:** 15 minutes

NUT-FREE, VEGETARIAN

4 cups water

Pinch sea salt

1 cup instant polenta

3 tablespoons tomato sauce

4½ ounces mozzarella, diced

1 cup cherry tomatoes, each cut in half

1 cup packed baby spinach

¼ to ½ cup mushrooms, diced

1 tablespoon dried oregano

2 tablespoons extra-virgin olive oil

1. Fill a pot with the water, add the salt, and bring to a boil over high heat. Add the polenta, lower the heat to medium, and whisk for 5 minutes, until the polenta starts to thicken. Cook for 5 more minutes, stirring frequently. Remove from the heat and let cool for 3 minutes.

2. Preheat the oven to 450°F. Line a baking sheet with parchment paper.

3. Transfer the polenta to a clean work surface, spread it out to 1-inch thick, and let it cool completely.

4. With a sharp knife, cut the polenta into 2½-inch, toddler-size squares and place them on the prepared baking sheet.

5. Spread ½ teaspoon tomato sauce on each square and top with a few pieces of mozzarella, 1 or 2 cherry tomatoes, 1 baby spinach leaf, 1 to 2 teaspoons diced mushrooms, and a sprinkle of oregano. Drizzle with olive oil.

continued

ADVANCED FINGER FOODS (12 MONTHS AND UP)

6. Bake for 5 minutes, until the mozzarella melts.

7. Cool and serve, refrigerate in an airtight container for up to 3 days, or freeze (before adding the toppings) for up to 3 months.

Preparation Tip: Transfer the polenta to a clean baking sheet and place in the refrigerator to speed up the cooling process.

104

SHRIMP AND AVOCADO SALAD

Caregivers tend to get stumped by or just plain old forget, how to offer their kids shellfish. Make it a priority to include fish or seafood in your child's diet at least two or three times per week once they have a few teeth to help chew the trickier texture. This recipe will help you easily incorporate shrimp into your meal rotation for a healthy dose of iodine and omega-3 fatty acids to promote brain development and exposure to common allergens.

Makes 8 servings | **Serving size:** ¼ cup
Prep time: 10 minutes | **Cook time:** 10 minutes

DAIRY-FREE, GLUTEN-FREE, NUT-FREE

3 tablespoons extra-virgin olive oil

2 garlic cloves, minced

1 teaspoon minced fresh parsley

1 pound raw shrimp

½ teaspoon sweet paprika

Pinch sea salt

4 Hass avocados, peeled, pitted, and diced, shells reserved

½ cup frozen corn, thawed

1. In a medium skillet over medium-high heat, warm the olive oil. Add the garlic and parsley and cook for 2 minutes. Add the shrimp, paprika, and salt and cook until the shrimp turn pink, about 4 minutes. Be careful not to overcook them. Turn off the heat and let the shrimp cool.

2. Add the avocado and corn and stir to combine.

3. To make it more toddler-friendly, cut the cooked shrimp into toddler-size bites and mash the avocado with a fork.

4. Spoon the salad into the avocado shells and serve.

Ingredient Tip: It's important to purchase high-quality shrimp to avoid any contamination. Avoid shrimp that appears to have black edges or spots and smells "fishy."

SMASHED-BEAN QUESADILLAS WITH EASY SALSA DIP

What kid doesn't like to dip and dunk? If your little one can't quite execute this skill yet, this quesadilla recipe is the perfect opportunity to let them practice and fuel their body with beneficial nutrients with each bite. Adding beans to the quesadilla is an easy way to pack in more protein, fiber, vitamins, and minerals. Let your toddler have some fun by helping smash the beans and sprinkling on the cheese.

Makes 16 servings | **Serving size:** ¼ quesadilla
Prep time: 5 minutes | **Cook time:** 10 minutes

NUT-FREE, VEGETARIAN

1 (14-ounce) can pinto or black beans, drained and rinsed

½ teaspoon chili powder

¼ teaspoon garlic powder

Pinch salt

1 to 2 tablespoons vegetable oil

4 (8- to 10-inch) whole-wheat tortillas

1. Preheat the oven to 400°F. Line a baking sheet with parchment paper or aluminum foil.

2. Place the beans in a large bowl and mash with a potato masher or the back of a fork. Stir in the chili powder, garlic powder, and a big pinch of salt. Set aside.

3. Use a pastry brush to paint a little oil all over one side of 2 tortillas. Place them oiled-side down on the prepared baking sheet. Sprinkle about ¼ cup shredded cheese over each tortilla. Add the mashed beans on top of the cheese, then divide the remaining ½ cup cheese on top of the beans. Place the remaining 2 tortillas on top and press down gently. Paint a little oil over the top tortillas.

1 cup shredded whole or part-skim cheddar cheese or Mexican cheese blend

½ cup jarred mild salsa

½ cup plain Greek yogurt

4. Bake until the tortillas are golden brown and the cheese is melted, about 10 minutes.

5. While the quesadillas are cooking, stir the salsa and yogurt together in a small bowl.

6. Let the quesadillas cool in the pan, then cut into wedges. Serve with the dipping sauce.

Preparation Tip: If you're pressed for time, skip the oven altogether and zap the quesadillas in the microwave until the cheese is melted. This will make a softer, less crunchy quesadilla, but it will still be delicious and it saves a little time.

CHICKEN PARM PASTA BAKE

Baked pasta dishes are my go-to dinner when I want something easy that will leave leftovers for tomorrow. I also like to pack pasta dishes with extra vegetables. Yes, the marinara sauce does count as vegetable exposure and provides a decent punch of vitamin C, but don't be afraid to throw in a few other vegetables to help clean out your refrigerator, plus add extra vitamins, minerals, and fiber. Sauté the additional veggies you want to use up and toss them in at step 3.

Makes 8 to 10 servings | **Serving size:** ½ cup
Prep time: 20 minutes | **Cook time:** 20 minutes

NUT-FREE

12 ounces whole-wheat fusilli or penne pasta (or any kind of pasta)

1 tablespoon extra-virgin olive oil, plus more for greasing

1 carrot

2 cups baby spinach (optional)

1 (24-ounce) jar marinara sauce

2 cups cooked chicken

1. Cook the pasta in salted boiling water according to the package directions. Drain and set aside.

2. Preheat the oven to 425°F. Grease a 9-by-13-inch baking dish with olive oil.

3. Peel the carrot, then shred it to yield about ½ cup finely grated carrots. Add it to a large bowl. Tear the spinach (if using) into smaller pieces and add to the carrots. Pour the marinara sauce over the vegetables in the bowl and stir to combine.

4. Shred the cooked chicken with your hands or chop it into small pieces. Add to the bowl with the veggies and sauce. Add the cooked pasta and 1 cup shredded mozzarella.

5. Stir the pasta and sauce, then transfer to the prepared pan and spread in an even layer.

2 cups shredded whole or part-skim mozzarella cheese, divided

½ cup panko bread crumbs

¼ cup grated Parmesan cheese

6. In a separate bowl, mix the remaining 1 cup shredded mozzarella, the panko bread crumbs, grated Parmesan cheese, and olive oil. Sprinkle over the top of the pasta in the baking dish.

7. Bake until the top is golden brown and the cheese is melted, 10 to 15 minutes.

8. Serve immediately, refrigerate in an airtight container for up to 3 days, or freeze for up to 3 months.

Good to Know: Make sure to reheat leftovers to a minimum of 165°F for at least 15 seconds to ensure it's safe to eat.

HOMEMADE YOYO-RANCH DIP

Everyone needs a good homemade ranch dip in their back pocket. This is easy enough to whip up on the fly and is guaranteed to help your toddler enjoy more veggies. Plus, this dip will provide more protein and less added sugar and sodium than store-bought versions. I'm all about increasing the nutritional value without jeopardizing the taste.

Makes 8 servings | **Serving size:** ¼ cup
Prep time: 5 minutes

GLUTEN-FREE, NUT-FREE, VEGETARIAN

1 lemon, halved

1½ cups full-fat or 2-percent plain Greek yogurt

½ cup mayonnaise (or more yogurt)

1 teaspoon dried dill

½ teaspoon onion powder

½ teaspoon garlic powder

½ teaspoon paprika

Pinch salt

1. Juice the lemon into a small bowl using a juicer or lemon squeezer.

2. Measure 2 tablespoons lemon juice into a larger bowl. Add the yogurt, mayonnaise, dill, onion powder, garlic powder, paprika, and salt. Use a whisk to slowly stir everything together. Serve this dip chilled with favorite crunchy veggies or anything else you like for dipping.

Preparation Tip: Let your toddler help scoop, stir, and sprinkle ingredients when you make this recipe. Before you know it, they'll be making it themselves.

MINI MEAT LOAVES

Meat loaf is a great way to offer multiple food groups so that your child gets a wide variety of nutrients. You can use your choice of ground meat in this recipe. The oats are a great whole-grain option to use instead of panko or regular bread crumbs, and adding veggies such as shredded zucchini or carrots is a no-brainer.

Makes 12 servings | **Serving size:** 2 mini meat loaves
Prep time: 10 minutes | **Cook time:** 20 minutes

DAIRY-FREE, GLUTEN-FREE, NUT-FREE

1 tablespoon olive oil, plus more for greasing

½ onion, roughly chopped

1 small zucchini, roughly chopped

1 pound ground meat

1 large egg

¼ cup old fashioned oats

1. Preheat the oven to 350°F.

2. Prepare a mini-muffin pan by lightly coating each cup with oil.

3. In a blender or food processor, blend the onion and zucchini until smooth. Transfer to a large bowl.

4. Add the meat, egg, oats, and oil. Use a potato masher to combine.

5. Using your hands or a tablespoon, scoop about 1 tablespoon of the mixture into each muffin well.

6. Bake for about 20 minutes, until the edges begin to brown and come away from the sides and the internal temperature reaches 165°F. If you are making full-size muffins, bake for an additional 10 minutes.

7. Serve immediately, refrigerate in an airtight container for up to 3 days, or freeze for up to 3 months.

Variation: Top the mini meat loaves with whichever mashed potato recipe you choose, and you instantly have meat loaf cupcakes!

ADVANCED FINGER FOODS (12 MONTHS AND UP)

HOMEMADE CHICKEN DUNKERS

All kids seem to love chicken fingers. If you're struggling to find something your toddler will love to eat that fuels their body optimally, give these homemade chicken fingers a whirl. You might find that your toddler eats more ketchup than you'd like, so try to rotate sauces and expose them to different flavors to dunk their chicken fingers in, such as the Homemade Yoyo-Ranch Dip on page 110.

Makes 10 to 12 servings | **Serving size:** 2 strips
Prep time: 10 minutes | **Cook time:** 25 minutes

DAIRY-FREE, NUT-FREE

Olive oil cooking spray (optional)

1½ cups panko bread crumbs (gluten-free bread crumbs optional)

½ teaspoon onion powder

Pinch salt

1 large egg

1 pound boneless, skinless chicken breast or thighs, cut into ½-inch-thick slices

1 tablespoon olive oil

1. Preheat the oven to 400°F.

2. Prepare a baking sheet by lining it with parchment paper or foil. If using foil, spray it with the cooking spray.

3. In a medium-size mixing bowl, combine the bread crumbs, onion powder, and salt. Then spread this mixture onto a plate or another baking sheet.

4. In another medium-size mixing bowl, beat the egg.

5. Place the chicken pieces in the bowl with the egg and toss to coat each piece.

6. Add each piece of chicken to the plate with the bread crumbs, then roll each piece to cover in the crumbs and seasoning.

7. Place the breaded chicken on the prepared baking sheet and coat with the olive oil.

8. Bake for 25 minutes, flipping halfway through. The internal temperature of the chicken should reach 165°F.

9. Serve immediately, refrigerate in an airtight container for up to 3 days, or freeze for up to 3 months.

Variation: Use this same recipe to quickly turn your homemade chicken dunkers into homemade chicken nuggets by simply cutting the chicken into bite-size pieces before breading. Voilà! Now you have two recipes you know your toddler will eat.

VEGGIE DUMPLINGS

Dumplings not only provide a great opportunity to incorporate vegetables, they're also a fun finger food for your toddler. Most toddlers will use their hands to eat, but try giving them an easy-to-hold utensil to practice with. If you really want to give them a challenge, offer a pair of chopsticks to play with. You can purchase child-appropriate chopsticks to make the task a bit more manageable.

Makes 16 servings | **Serving size:** 2 dumplings
Prep time: 15 minutes | **Cook time:** 15 minutes

DAIRY-FREE, NUT-FREE, VEGETARIAN

1 tablespoon olive oil

1 garlic clove, chopped, or 1 teaspoon of jarred minced garlic

4 cups shredded cabbage and carrots

10 green onions, chopped

1 teaspoon sesame oil

2 tablespoons low-sodium soy sauce

1 package wonton wraps (at least 32 wrappers)

1. Using a large nonstick pan or wok, heat the oil over medium heat, then sauté the garlic and the cabbage-and-carrot blend until the cabbage begins to shrink, 2 to 3 minutes.

2. Add the green onions, sesame oil, and soy sauce. Continue to cook for about 5 minutes, until the liquid begins to evaporate.

3. Remove the pan from the stovetop and set aside.

4. Fill each wonton wrap with some of the mixture. Follow the dumpling folding instructions on the package. It may take a few tries to get it right.

5. Boil a large pot of water. When the water comes to a rolling boil, cook the dumplings, about 8 at a time, until they are cooked through, 3 to 4 minutes.

6. Use a slotted spoon to remove the dumplings and set on a plate, but don't let the baby touch while it's still hot.

7. Cool and serve, or space them out in an airtight container and refrigerate for up to 3 days or freeze for up to 3 months.

Variation: Consider adding 1 tablespoon of finely grated ginger in step 1, or add 2 cups of shiitake mushrooms, chopped, in step 2 to change these dumplings up a bit.

BAKED MACARONI AND CHEESE CUPS

I use this kid-friendly recipe to make veggies a little more inviting. Provide your toddler with two veggie options and let them pick which one will go into the macaroni cups. This creates owner-ship and autonomy and is helpful when mealtime comes around and it's time for your child to try it.

Makes 12 servings | **Serving size:** 1 muffin
Prep time: 10 minutes | **Cook time:** 25 minutes

NUT-FREE, VEGETARIAN

½ **cup bread crumbs (gluten-free bread crumbs optional)**

1 **tablespoon unsalted butter, melted**

1 **garlic clove, minced**

1 **tablespoon chopped fresh parsley**

4 **cups shredded cheese**

4 **tablespoons all-purpose flour (gluten-free flour optional)**

Pinch salt

Pinch black pepper

1. Preheat the oven to 375°F.

2. In a small bowl, combine the bread crumbs, melted butter, garlic, and parsley. Set aside.

3. In a medium bowl, combine the cheese, flour, salt, and pepper, tossing to mix.

4. In a medium saucepan, bring the cream, milk, and mustard to a gentle boil, stirring often.

5. Add the cheese mixture to the cream mixture. Mix well and cook until the cheese is melted and the mixture is bubbly.

6. Remove the saucepan from the heat, then add the cooked mac-aroni to the cheese sauce. Stir to mix and let rest for 5 minutes.

7. Place silicone liners into a muffin tin. Spoon the macaroni mix-ture into the muffin cups and top with the bread crumb mixture.

1 cup heavy
   (whipping) cream

1 cup milk

¼ teaspoon dry mustard

8 ounces elbow maca-
   roni, cooked al dente
   (gluten-free pasta
   optional)

8. Bake the cups for 10 to 15 minutes, or until the cheese sauce is bubbly and the bread crumbs are browned.

9. Serve immediately, refrigerate in an airtight container for up to 3 days, or freeze for up to 3 months. When reheating, add a little milk to make it creamy again.

Variation: My family occasionally enjoys macaroni and cheese from a box, and sometimes we end up with leftovers. This is a great opportunity to turn the leftovers into mac 'n' cheese cups. Add a little milk to thin it out, along with some bread crumbs to help hold it together, and proceed with step 7.

GOOEY AVOCADO GRILLED CHEESE

Even my husband gets excited about this recipe, and it's likely to be one of your baby's favorites, too. Grilled cheese is an easy favorite for many kids, making it a great vessel for fruits and veggies—hence the avocado. The creaminess of the avocado blends well with the gooiness of the cheese, and the crunch of the toasty bread makes for three food groups all in one.

Makes 4 servings | **Serving size:** ¼ sandwich
Prep time: 5 minutes | **Cook time:** 10 minutes

NUT-FREE, VEGETARIAN

2 slices bread

1 tablespoon unsalted butter, at room temperature

½ ripe avocado, peeled and mashed

2 ounces shredded cheddar cheese (about ½ cup)

1. Heat a medium cast-iron skillet over medium heat.

2. Spread one side of each bread slice with butter. Place one slice of bread buttered-side down in the skillet.

3. Spread the avocado on the slice in the skillet and top it with the cheese and the remaining slice of bread, buttered-side up. Cook for about 5 minutes, or until the bottom side of the bread is golden brown. Flip and cook on the other side for 3 to 5 minutes, until the bread is golden brown and the cheese has melted.

4. Transfer the sandwich to a cutting board and allow it to cool before slicing it into strips or wedges for baby.

Ingredient Tip: When choosing bread, aim for a whole-grain bread to get more vitamins, minerals, and fiber. Look for the word "whole" within the first two ingredients. Avoid breads with nuts and seeds, which can be a choking hazard.

Pairing Tip: Pairing this grilled cheese with Creamy Tomato Soup (page 73) is a no-brainer.

118

Measurement Conversions

	US STANDARD	US STANDARD (OUNCES)	METRIC (APPROXIMATE)
VOLUME EQUIVALENTS (LIQUID)	2 tablespoons	1 fl. oz.	30 mL
	¼ cup	2 fl. oz.	60 mL
	½ cup	4 fl. oz.	120 mL
	1 cup	8 fl. oz.	240 mL
	1½ cups	12 fl. oz.	355 mL
	2 cups or 1 pint	16 fl. oz.	475 mL
	4 cups or 1 quart	32 fl. oz.	1 L
	1 gallon	128 fl. oz.	4 L
VOLUME EQUIVALENTS (DRY)	⅛ teaspoon	————	0.5 mL
	¼ teaspoon	————	1 mL
	½ teaspoon	————	2 mL
	¾ teaspoon	————	4 mL
	1 teaspoon	————	5 mL
	1 tablespoon	————	15 mL
	¼ cup	————	59 mL
	⅓ cup	————	79 mL
	½ cup	————	118 mL
	⅔ cup	————	156 mL
	¾ cup	————	177 mL
	1 cup	————	235 mL
	2 cups or 1 pint	————	475 mL
	3 cups	————	700 mL
	4 cups or 1 quart	————	1 L
	½ gallon	————	2 L
	1 gallon	————	4 L
WEIGHT EQUIVALENTS	½ ounce	————	15 g
	1 ounce	————	30 g
	2 ounces	————	60 g
	4 ounces	————	115 g
	8 ounces	————	225 g
	12 ounces	————	340 g
	16 ounces or 1 pound	————	455 g

Resources

These are some of my favorite products that make mealtimes easier for me and my children. You don't need much, but by providing your children with the right tools, you can help them be successful eaters with happy bellies.

High chair: Abiie Beyond Junior Y High Chair for an adjustable, easy to clean high chair that grows with your child.

Infant utensils: eZtotZ Small Hands Baby Utensils Ergonomic Spoon and Fork Set and their Little Dippers Starter Spoon & Teether make self-feeding fun and easy.

Open cups: A simple medicine cup or eZtotZ My First Cup helps your baby learn how to master drinking from an open cup.

Straw cups: The First Years Take & Toss Spill-Proof Straw Cups or the Munchkin Any Angle Click Lock Weighted Straw Trainer Cup for times when you want less mess and are on the go.

Suction plates: Bumkins Silicone Grip Dish Suction Plates decrease plate throwing.

Popsicle Molds: Nuby Garden Fresh Fruitsicle Frozen Pop Tray to make nutrient-dense popsicles.

If you have more questions about how to care for your baby, visit HealthyChildren.org for reliable information from the American Academy of Pediatrics.

References

American Academy of Pediatrics. "Botulism." Accessed November 29, 2020. HealthyChildren .org/English/health-issues/conditions/infections/Pages/Botulism.aspx.

American Academy of Pediatrics. "Starting Solid Foods." Accessed November 28, 2020. HealthyChildren.org/English/ages-stages/baby/feeding-nutrition/Pages/Starting-Solid-Foods.aspx.

American Academy of Pediatrics. "Tips for Introducing Solid Foods." Accessed November 28, 2020. HealthyChildren.org/English/ages-stages/baby/feeding-nutrition/Pages/Tips-for-Introducing-Solid -Foods.aspx.

American Academy of Pediatrics. "Why Formula Instead of Cow's Milk?" Accessed November 26, 2020. HealthyChildren.org/English/ages-stages/baby/formula-feeding/Pages/Why-Formula -Instead-of-Cows-Milk.aspx.

Brown, Lee A., MD. "Early Influences on Child Satiety-Responsiveness: The Role of Weaning Style." *Pediatr Obes.* 2015 Feb;10(1):57–66. DOI:10.1111/j.2047-6310.2013.00207.x. Epub 2013 Dec 17. PMID: 24347496.

Brown, Lee A., MD. "Maternal Control of Child Feeding during the Weaning Period: Differences between Mothers Following a Baby-Led or Standard Weaning Approach." *Maternal Child Health Journal.* 2011 Nov;15(8):1265–71. DOI:10.1007/s10995-010-0678-4. PMID: 20830511.

Cameron, S. L., A. L. Heath, and R. W. Taylor. "How Feasible is Baby-led Weaning as an Approach to Infant Feeding? A Review of the Evidence." *Nutrients.* 2012 Nov 2;4(11):1575–609. DOI:10.3390 /nu4111575. PMID: 23201835; PMCID: PMC3509508.

Centers for Disease Control and Prevention. "Milestone Moments." Accessed November 26, 2020. CDC.gov/ncbddd/actearly/pdf/parents_pdfs/milestonemomentseng508.pdf.

Centers for Disease Control and Prevention. "When, What, and How to Introduce Solid Foods." Accessed November 28, 2020. CDC.gov/nutrition/infantandtoddlernutrition/foods-and -drinks/when-to-introduce-solid-foods.html.

Chang, J. S., K.C. Wang, C.F. Yeh, D.E. Shieh, and L.C. Chiang. "Fresh Ginger (Zingiber Officinale) Has Anti-viral Activity against Human Respiratory Syncytial Virus in Human Respiratory Tract Cell Lines." *J Ethnopharmacol.* 2013 Jan 9;145(1):146–51. DOI:10.1016/j.jep.2012.10.043. Epub 2012 Nov 1. PMID: 23123794.

Food Allergy Research & Education. "Learning Early About Peanut Allergy (LEAP)." Accessed November 29, 2020. FoodAllergy.org/resources/learning-early-about-peanut-allergy-leap.

Hammons, AJ, and BH Fiese. "Is Frequency of Shared Family Meals Related to the Nutritional Health of Children and Adolescents?" *Pediatrics.* 2011 Jun;127(6):e1565–74. DOI:10.1542 /peds.2010-1440. Epub 2011 May 2. PMID: 21536618; PMCID: PMC3387875.

Hosomi, R, M Yoshida, and K Fukunaga. "Seafood Consumption and Components for Health." *Glob J Health Sci.* 2012 Apr 28;4(3):72–86. DOI:10.5539/gjhs.v4n3p72. PMID: 22980234; PMCID: PMC4776937.

Immune Tolerance Network. "LEAP Study Results." Accessed November 29, 2020. LEAPStudy .co.uk/leap-0#.X-IgzthKhPZ.

National CACFP Association. "Stages of Infant Development and Feeding Skills." Accessed November 26, 2020. KNCInc.org/wp-content/uploads/2019/08/developmental-stages -training08062019.pdf.

U.S. Food and Drug Administration. "Advice about Eating Fish." Accessed December 6, 2020. FDA. gov/food/consumers/advice-about-eating-fish.

Index

127

INDEX

131

Acknowledgments

As a dietitian, it's always been on my bucket list to write a book. I never thought that I'd accomplish this within my first five years as a professional, let alone with two toddlers running around at home and working full time.

A huge thank you to my parents for prioritizing family meals, vegetables—even when canned—and traditions around the food we love to enjoy. Thank you for teaching me how to love both ice cream and broccoli.

Thank you to my Instagram community, who have supported me in educating parents on how to feed their families in a realistic way.

None of this would have been possible without my amazing husband. Thank you for taking our children on random car rides and errands just so I could have alone time to write this book. You're the best husband and I love you for all that you do for our family.

About the Author

ALEXANDRA TURNBULL, RDN, LD is a registered dietitian, top 20 nutrition influencer, founder of The Family Nutritionist and, most important, a mom. She works full time as a dietitian in school food service, where she helps fuel thousands of students on a daily basis. On the side, she manages The Family Nutritionist, where she helps parents feed their families with more confidence and less stress. Alex combines a research-based approach with real-world experience as a mom of two little ones to help educate parents and caregivers on how to safely introduce solids and cut down on mealtime battles.

Born and raised in Minnesota, you-betcha she's spending her summer at the lake and thoroughly enjoying every snowflake at Christmas. She still lives in Minnesota with her husband, Blaine, daughter, Brexley, son, Hollis, and Malti-poo, Mia. Her favorite foods and beverages are cheeseburgers, roasted broccoli, coffee, and wine—definitely coffee and wine.

CPSIA information can be obtained
at www.ICGtesting.com
Printed in the USA
JSHW011357280621
16148JS00005B/7

9 781648 769351